MORE INS

RUSS ULMER

Insights Publishing
www.insightsonlife.net

Much of the material in Insights books is by unknown authors, has been contributed by readers and is presented here with the spirit of sharing for strict personal use: with friends, family, or co-workers--to pass it on. Insights Publishing attempts to attribute all credits, where available, to material in this book.

ISBN 978-0-9793313-4-3

First Printing 2009

Printed in the USA by Insights Publishing
www.insightsonlife.net

I would like to
dedicate this book to all those
that live life to it’s fullest.
Enjoy life!

Other Books Available
From Russ Ulmer

Insights on Life
Insights on Attitude
Insights on Nursing Humor
Insights for Mothers

CONTENTS

INTRODUCTION

As with my previous *Insights on Life* book, all of the selections for this book are by unknown authors. I will give credit to the original author if they come forward or if someone can provide that information to me. Most of the contributions were from those of you that have read the first edition (thank you). Others were those that I had left out of the original.

I would like to give a word of thanks to those that purchased *Insights on Life*. Although it did not make the New York Times Bestseller list I was very pleased with its modest sales and especially by the feedback I received by its readers.

Enjoy Life!

-1-

LIFE

The life which is unexamined is not worth living.
- Plato

Life is a sexually transmitted disease.
Anonymous

WITH A FORK
AUTHOR UNKNOWN

There was a woman who had been diagnosed with cancer and had been given 3 months to live. Her Dr. told her to start making preparations to die. So she contacted her pastor and had him come to her house to discuss certain aspects of her final wishes. She told him which songs she wanted sung at the service, what scriptures she would like read, and what she wanted to be wearing.

The woman also told her pastor that she wanted to be buried with her favorite bible. Everything was in order and the pastor was preparing to leave when the woman suddenly remembered something very important to her.
"There's one more thing" she said excitedly. "What's that?" came the pastor's reply. "This is very important." The woman continued. "I want to be buried with a fork in my right hand." The pastor stood looking at the woman not knowing quite what to say. "That shocks you doesn't it?" the woman asked. "Well to be honest, I'm puzzled by the request" said the pastor.

The woman explained. "In all my years of attending church socials and functions where food was involved (and let's be honest, food is an important part of any church event; spiritual or otherwise); my favorite was when whoever was clearing away the dishes of the main course would lean over and say "you can keep your fork."

The pastor's eyes were welled up with tears of joy as he hugged the woman goodbye. He knew this would be one of the last times he would see her before her death. But he also knew that the woman had a better grasp of heaven than he did. She KNEW that something better was coming.

At the funeral people were walking by the woman's casket and they saw the pretty dress she was wearing and her favorite bible and the fork placed in her right hand. Over and over the pastor heard the question "What's with the fork?" And over and over he smiled.

During his message the pastor told the people of the conversation he had with the woman shortly before she died. He also told them about the fork and about what it symbolized to her. The pastor told the people how he could not stop thinking about the fork and told them that they probably would not be able to stop thinking about it either.

He was right. So the next time you reach down for your fork, let it remind you oh so gently that there is something better coming.

You're alive. Do something. The directive in life, the moral imperative was so uncomplicated. It could be expressed in single words, not complete sentences.
It sounded like this: Look. Listen. Choose. Act.
Barbara Hall

DECIDING
AUTHOR UNKNOWN

Outside my window, a new day I see,
And only I can determine
What kind of day it will be.
It can be busy and sunny, laughing and gay,
Or boring and cold, unhappy and gray.
My own state of mind is the determining key,
For I am only the person I let myself be.
I can be thoughtful and do all I can to help,
Or be selfish and think just of myself.
I can enjoy what I do and make it seem fun,
Or gripe and complain and make it hard on someone.
I can be patient with those who may not understand
Or belittle and hurt them as much as I can.
But I have faith in myself,
And believe what I say
And I personally intend to make the most of each day.

Not a shred of evidence exists in favor of the idea that life is serious.
Brendan Gill

PRESENT VALUE

AUTHOR UNKNOWN

Imagine there is a bank that credits your account each morning with $86,400. It carries over no balance from day to day. Every evening deletes whatever part of the balance you failed to use during the day.

What would you do? Draw out every cent, of course!!!! Each of us has such a bank. Its name is TIME.

Every morning, it credits you with 86,400 seconds. Every night it writes off, as lost, whatever of this you have failed to invest to good purpose. It carries over no balance. It allows no overdraft. Each day it opens a new account for you. Each night it burns the remains of the day. If you fail to use the day's deposits, the loss is yours.

There is no going back. There is no drawing against the "tomorrow". You must live in the present on today's deposits. Invest it so as to get from it the utmost in health, happiness, and success!

The clock is running. Make the most of today.

To realize the value of ONE YEAR, ask a student who failed a grade.
To realize the value of ONE MONTH, ask a mother who gave birth to a premature baby.
To realize the value of ONE WEEK, ask the editor of a weekly newspaper. .
To realize the value of ONE HOUR, ask the lovers who are waiting to meet.
To realize the value of ONE MINUTE, ask a person who missed the train.
To realize the value of ONE SECOND, ask a person who just avoided an accident.

To realize the value of ONE MILLISECOND, ask the person who won a silver medal in the Olympics.

Treasure every moment that you have! And treasure it more because you shared it with someone special, special enough to spend your time. And remember that time waits for no one.

Life is a foreign language; all men mispronounce it.
Christopher Morley

TAKE TIME

AUTHOR UNKNOWN

Take time to work; it is the price of success.

Take time to think; it is the source of power.

Take time to play; it is the secret of perpetual youth.

Take time to read; it is the foundation of wisdom.

Take time to be friendly; it is the road to happiness.

Take time to love and to be loved; it is the privilege of gods.

Take time to share; life is too short to be selfish.

Take time to laugh; laughter is the music of the soul.

The purpose of life is to fight maturity.
Dick Werthimer

THOUGHTS TO LIVE BY
AUTHOR UNKNOWN

Accept that some days you're the pigeon, and some days you're the statue.

Always keep your words soft and sweet, just in case you have to eat them.

Always read stuff that will make you look good if you die in the middle of it.

Be wary of strong drink. It can make you shoot at tax collectors, and miss.

Drive carefully. It's not only cars that can be recalled by their maker.

Eat a live toad in the morning and nothing worse will happen to you for the rest of the day.

If life gives you lemons, squeeze the juice into a watergun and shoot other people in the eyes.

If you can't be kind, at least have the decency to be vague.

If you can't beat your computer at chess, try kickboxing.

If you lend someone $20, and never see that person again, it was probably worth it.

If you try and don't succeed, cheat. Repeat until caught. Then lie.

It may be that your sole purpose in life is simply to serve as a warning to others.

Never buy a car you can't push.

Never put both feet in your mouth at the same time, because then you don't have a leg to stand on.

Never try to teach a pig to sing. It wastes your time and annoys the pig.

Nobody cares if you can't dance well. Just get up and dance.

The early worm gets eaten by the bird, so sleep late.

When everything's coming your way, you're in the wrong lane.

You are what you eat. So stay away from the jerk chicken.

Be nice to the nerds and geeks in high school -- you'll be working for them in the future.

Oh, life is a glorious cycle of song,
A medley of extemporanea;
And love is a thing that can never go wrong;
And I am Marie of Roumania.
Dorothy Parker

GREAT TRUTHS ABOUT LIFE THAT ADULTS HAVE LEARNED:

AUTHOR UNKNOWN

Raising teenagers is like nailing Jell-O to a tree.

Wrinkles don't hurt.

Families are like fudge...mostly sweet, with a few nuts.

Today's mighty oak is just yesterday's nut that held its ground.

Laughing is good exercise. It's like jogging on the inside.

Middle age is when you choose your cereal for the fiber, not the joy.

Life is just one damned thing after another.
Elbert Hubbard

THE FOUR STAGES OF LIFE

AUTHOR UNKNOWN

1) You believe in Santa Claus.
2) You don't believe in Santa Claus.
3) You are Santa Claus.
4) You look like Santa Claus.

Life is something that happens when you can't get to sleep.
Fran Lebowitz

THE POSITIVE SIDE OF LIFE

AUTHOR UNKNOWN

Living on Earth is expensive, but it does include a free trip around the sun every year.

How long a minute is depends on what side of the bathroom door you're on.

Birthdays are good for you; the more you have, the longer you live.

Happiness comes through doors you didn't even know you left open.

Ever notice that the people who are late are often much jollier than the people who have to wait for them?

Most of us go to our grave with our music still inside of us.

You may be only one person in the world, but you may also be the world to one person.

Some mistakes are too much fun to only make once.

Don't cry because it's over; smile because it happened.

We could learn a lot from crayons: some are sharp, some are pretty, some are dull, some have weird names, and all are different colors....but they all exist very nicely in the same box.

A truly happy person is one who can enjoy the scenery on a detour.

Life is something that everyone should try at least once.
Henry J. Tillman

THE LITTLE THINGS

AUTHOR UNKNOWN

Too often we don't realize
what we have until it is gone;
Too often we wait too late to say
"I'm sorry - I was wrong."

Sometimes it seems we hurt the ones
we hold dearest to our hearts;
And we allow foolish things
to tear our lives apart.

Far too many times we let
unimportant things into our minds;
And then it's usually too late
to see what made us blind.

So be sure that you let people know
how much they mean to you;
Take that time to say the words
before your time is through.

Be sure that you appreciate
everything you've got
And be thankful for the
little things in life
that mean a lot.

-2-

CHILDREN

It's fun being a kid.
Bradford Arthur Angier

GREAT TRUTHS ABOUT LIFE THAT LITTLE CHILDREN HAVE LEARNED:

AUTHOR UNKNOWN

No matter how hard you try, you can't baptize cats.

When your Mom is mad at your Dad, don't let her brush your hair.

If your sister hits you, don't hit her back. They always catch the second person.

You can't trust dogs to watch your food.

Don't sneeze when someone is cutting your hair.

Never hold a Dust-Buster and a cat at the same time.

You can't hide a piece of broccoli in a glass of milk.

Don't wear polka-dot underwear under white shorts.

The best place to be when you're sad is Grandpa's lap.

It is amazing how quickly the kids learn to drive a car, yet are unable to understand the lawnmower, snow-blower, or vacuum cleaner.
Ben Bergor

RESIGNATION
AUTHOR UNKNOWN

I am hereby officially tendering my resignation as an adult. I have decided I would like to accept the responsibilities of an 8 year-old again.

I want to go to McDonald's and think that it's a four star restaurant.

I want to sail sticks across a fresh mud puddle and make a sidewalk with rocks.

I want to think M&Ms are better than money because you can eat them.

I want to lie under a big oak tree and run a lemonade stand with my friends on a hot summer's day.

I want to return to a time when life was simple; When all you knew were colors, multiplication tables, and nursery rhymes, but that didn't bother you, because you didn't know what you didn't know and you didn't care.

All you knew was to be happy because you were blissfully unaware of all the things that should make you worried or upset.

I want to think the world is fair. That everyone is honest and good.

I want to believe that anything is possible. I want to be oblivious to the complexities of life and be overly excited by the little things again.

I want to live simple again. I don't want my day to consist of computer crashes, mountains of paperwork, depressing news, how to survive more days in the month than there is money in the bank, doctor bills, gossip, illness, and loss of loved ones.

I want to believe in the power of smiles, hugs, a kind word, truth, justice, peace, dreams, the imagination, mankind, and making angels in the snow.

So . .. here's my checkbook and my car-keys, my credit card bills and my 401K statements. I am officially resigning from adulthood.

And if you want to discuss this further, you'll have to catch me first, cause........ ......"Tag! You're it."

Pass this to someone and brighten their day by helping them remember the Simple things in Life.

The only moral lesson which is suited for a child, the most important lesson for every time of life, is this: "Never hurt anybody."

Denis Breeze

LUNCH IN THE PARK

AUTHOR UNKNOWN

There once was a little boy who wanted to meet God. He knew it was a long trip to where God lived, so he packed his suitcase with Twinkies and a six pack of root beer and he started his journey.

When he had gone about three blocks, he met an old woman. She was sitting in the park just staring at some pigeons. The boy sat down next to her and opened his suitcase.

He was about to take a drink from his root beer when he noticed that the old lady looked hungry, so he offered her a Twinkie. She gratefully accepted it and smiled at him. Her smile was so pretty that the boy wanted to see it again, so he offered her a root beer.

Once again she smiled at him. The boy was delighted! They sat there all afternoon eating and smiling, but they never said a word.

As it grew dark, the boy realized how tired he was and he got up to leave, but before he had gone more than a few steps, he turned around, ran back to the old woman and gave her a hug. She gave him her biggest smile ever.

When the boy opened the door to his own house a short time later, his mother was surprised by the look of joy on his face.

She asked him, "What did you do today that made you so happy?" He replied, "I had lunch with God."

But before his mother could respond, he added, "You know what? She's got the most beautiful smile I've ever seen!"

Meanwhile, the old woman, also radiant with joy, returned to her home.
Her son was stunned by the look of peace on her face and he asked, "Mother, what did you do today that made you so happy?" She replied, "I ate Twinkies in the park with God."

But before her son responded, she added, "You know, he's much younger than I expected."

To be ignorant of what occurred before you were born is to remain always a child.
Marcus T. Cicero

CHILDRENS 10 COMMANDMENTS

AUTHOR UNKNOWN

1. My hands are small; please don't expect perfection whenever I make my bed, draw a picture or throw a ball. My legs are short; please slow down so that I can keep up with you.

2. My eyes have not seen the world as yours have; please let me explore safely; don't restrict me unnecessarily.

3. Housework will always be there. I'm only little for such a short time- please take the time to explain things to me about this wonderful world and do so willingly.

4. My feelings are tender; please be sensitive to my needs; don't nag me all day long. (You wouldn't want to be nagged for your inquisitiveness). Treat me as you would like to be treated.

5. I am a special gift; please treasure me as
my Creator intended you to do, holding me accountable for my actions, giving me guidelines to live by and disciplining me in a loving manner.

6. I need your encouragement, not just your praise to grow. Please go easy on the criticism;
you can criticize the things I do without criticizing me.

7. Please give me the freedom to make decisions concerning myself. Permit me to fail, so that I can learn from my own mistakes. Then someday I will be prepared to make the kind of decisions life will require of me.

8. Please don't do things over for me. Somehow that makes me feel that my efforts didn't quite measure to your expectations. I know it's hard, but please don't try to compare me to my brother or sister.

9. Please don't be afraid to leave for a weekend together. Kids need a vacation from parents, just as parents need vacations from kids. Besides it's a great way to show us kids that your marriage is very special.

10. Please set a good example for me to follow in all the ways of life. I enjoy watching the things you do and want to do them just like you do.

-3-

LEARNING

Learning is not attained by chance. It must be sought for with ardor and attended to with diligence.
Abigail Adams

THE HAND

AUTHOR UNKNOWN

The first grade teacher gave her class a fun assignment -- to draw a picture of something for which they were thankful. Most of the class might be considered economically disadvantaged, but still many would have things that they were thankful for. But Douglas made a different kind of picture.

Douglas was a different kind of boy. He was the teacher's true child of misery, frail and unhappy. As other children played at recess, Douglas was likely to stand close by her side. One could only guess at the pain Douglas felt behind those sad eyes.

Yes, his picture was different. When asked to draw a picture of something for which he was thankful, he drew a hand. Nothing else. Just an empty hand. His abstract image captured the imagination of his peers. Whose hand could it be? One child guessed it was the hand of a farmer, because farmers raised food. Another suggested a police officer, because the police protect and care for people. Still others guessed it was the hand of God, for God feeds us. And so the discussion went-until the teacher almost forgot the young artist himself.

When the children had gone on to other assignments, she paused at Douglas' desk, bent down, and asked him whose hand it was. The little boy looked away and murmured, "It's yours, teacher." She recalled the times she had taken his hand and walked with him here or there, as she had the other students. How often had she said, "Take my hand, Douglas, we'll go outside." Or, "Let me show you how to hold your pencil." Or, "Let's do this together." Douglas was most thankful for his teacher's hand. Brushing aside a tear, she went on with her work.

The story speaks of more than thankfulness. It says something about teachers teaching and parents parenting and friends showing friendship, and how much it means to the Douglases of the world. They might not always say thanks. But they'll remember the hand that reaches out.

It is always in season for old men to learn.
Aeschylus

I'VE LEARNED

AUTHOR UNKNOWN

I've learned-
that no matter how much I care,
some people just don't care back.

I've learned-
that it takes years to build up trust,
and only seconds to destroy it.

I've learned-
that it's not what you have in your life
but who you have in your life that counts.

I've learned-
that you can get by on charm
for about fifteen minutes.
After that, you'd better know something.

I've learned-
that you shouldn't compare
yourself to the best others can do.

I've learned-
that you can do something in an instant
that will give you heartache for life.

I've learned-
that it's taking me a long time
to become the person I want to be.

I've learned-
that you should always leave loved ones
with loving words. It may be the last
time you see them.

I've learned-
that you can keep going
long after you think you can't.

I've learned-
that we are responsible for what we do,
no matter how we feel.

I've learned-
that either you control your attitude
or it controls you.

I've learned-
that regardless of how hot and steamy
a relationship is at first, the passion fades
and there had better be something else
to take its place.

I've learned-
that heroes are the people
who do what has to be done
when it needs to be done,
regardless of the consequences.

I've learned-
that money is a lousy way of keeping score.

I've learned-
that my best friend and I can do anything
or nothing and have the best time.

I've learned-
that sometimes the people you expect
to kick you when you're down
will be the ones to help you get back up.

I've learned-
that sometimes when I'm angry
I have the right to be angry,
but that doesn't give me the right to be cruel.

I've learned-
that true friendship continues to grow,
even over the longest distance.
Same goes for true love.

I've learned-
that just because someone doesn't love
you the way you want them to doesn't
mean they don't love you with all they have.

I've learned-
that maturity has more to do with
what types of experiences you've had
and what you've learned from them
and less to do with how many
birthdays you've celebrated.

I've learned-
that you should never tell a child
their dreams are unlikely or outlandish.
Few things are more humiliating, and what
a tragedy it would be if they believed it.

I've learned-
that your family won't always be there for you.
It may seem funny, but people you aren't
related to can take care of you and love you

and teach you to trust people again.
Families aren't biological.

I've learned-
that no matter how good a friend is,
they're going to hurt you every once in a while
and you must forgive them for that.

I've learned-
that it isn't always enough to be forgiven by others.
Sometimes you are to learn to forgive yourself.

I've learned-
that no matter how bad your heart is broken
the world doesn't stop for your grief.

I've learned-
that our background and circumstances
may have influenced who we are,
but we are responsible for who we become.

I've learned-
that just because two people argue,
it doesn't mean they don't love each other
And just because they don't argue,
it doesn't mean they do.

I've learned-
that we don't have to change friends
if we understand that friends change.

I've learned-
that you shouldn't be so eager to find out a
secret. It could change your life forever.

I've learned-
that two people can look at the exact same thing
and see something totally different.

I've learned-
that no matter how you try to protect your
children, they will eventually get hurt and
you will hurt in the process.

I've learned-
that your life can be changed in a matter of
hours by people who don't even know you.

I've learned-
that even when you think you have no more
to give, when a friend cries out to you,
you will find the strength to help.

I've learned-
that the people you care about most in life
are taken from you too soon.

I've learned-
that it's hard to determine where to draw
the line between being nice and not hurting
people's feelings and standing up for what you believe.

-4-

PRENTHOOD

My parents only had one argument in forty-five years. It lasted forty-three years.
Cathy Ladman

1ST, 2ND, AND 3RD KID
AUTHOR UNKNOWN

Being a parent changes everything. But being a parent also changes with each baby. Here are some of the ways having a second and third child is different from having your first.

YOUR CLOTHES
1st baby: You begin wearing maternity clothes as soon as your OB/GYN confirms your pregnancy.
2nd baby: You wear your regular clothes for as long as possible.
3rd baby: Your maternity clothes ARE your regular clothes.

PREPARING FOR THE BIRTH
1st baby: You practice your breathing religiously.
2nd baby: You don't bother practicing because you remember that last time, breathing didn't do a thing.
3rd baby: You ask for an epidural in your 8th month.

THE NURSERY
1st baby: You pre-wash your newborn's clothes, color-coordinate them, and fold them neatly in the baby's little bureau.
2nd baby: You check to make sure that the clothes are clean and discard only the ones with the darkest stains.
3rd baby: Boys can wear pink, can't they?

WORRIES
1st baby: At the first sign of distress - a whimper, a frown-you pick up the baby.
2nd baby: You pick the baby up when her wails threaten to wake your first born.
3rd baby: You teach your 3-year-old how to rewind the mechanical swing.

PACIFIER
1st baby: If the pacifier falls on the floor, you put it away until you can go home and wash and boil it.
2nd baby: When the pacifier falls on the floor, you squirt it off with some juice from the baby's bottle.
3rd baby: You wipe it off on your shirt and pop it back in.

DIAPERING
1st baby: You change your baby's diapers every hour, whether they need it or not.
2nd baby: You change their diaper every 2 to 3 hours, if needed.
3rd baby: You try to change their diaper before others start to complain about the smell or you see it sagging to their knees.

ACTIVITIES
1st baby: You take your infant to Baby Gymnastics, Baby Swing, and Baby Story Hour.
2nd baby: You take your infant to Baby Gymnastics.
3rd baby: You take your infant to the supermarket and the dry cleaner.

GOING OUT
1st baby: The first time you leave your baby with a sitter, you call home 5 times.
2nd baby: Just before you walk out the door, you remember to leave a number

where you can be reached.
3rd baby: You leave instructions for the sitter to call only if she sees blood.

AT HOME
1st baby: You spend a good bit of every day just gazing at the baby.
2nd baby: You spend a bit of everyday watching to be sure your older child isn't squeezing, poking, or hitting the baby.
3rd baby: You spend a little bit of every day hiding from the children.

SWALLOWING COINS
1st child: when first child swallows a coin, you rush the child to the hospital and demand x-rays.
2nd child: when 2nd child swallows a coin, you carefully watch for coin to pass.
3rd child: when 3rd child swallows a coin you deduct it from his allowance!!

The first half of our lives is ruined by our parents, and the second half by our children.
Clarence Darrow

100 WAYS TO PRAISE A CHILD

AUTHOR UNKNOWN

WOW
NEAT
GOOD
GREAT
BRAVO
SUPER
A+ JOB
AWESOME
RADICAL
TERRIFIC
PERFECT
HOW NICE
DYNAMITE
GOOD JOB
GOOD STUFF
YOU CARE
MARVELOUS
HOW SMART
FANTASTIC
SUPERSTAR
EXCELLENT
WELL DONE

WAY TO GO
BEAUTIFUL
HOT STUFF
NICE WORK
SUPER JOB
PHENOMENAL
SUPER WORK
YOU BELONG
I LIKE YOU
THAT'S HOT
MAGNIFICENT
OUTSTANDING
I TRUST YOU
SPECTACULAR
GOOD FOR YOU
LOOKING GOOD
YOU'RE ON IT
TRY YOUR BEST
I RESPECT YOU
FANTASTIC JOB
YOU'RE UNIQUE
GOOD THINKING
CREATIVE WORK
BEAUTIFUL WORK
HURRAY FOR YOU
YOU TRIED HARD
YOU'RE SPECIAL
YOU'RE PERFECT

YOU'RE DARLING
REMARKABLE JOB
THAT'S CORRECT
YOU'RE THE BEST
YOU'RE SO SMART
GREAT DISCOVERY
YOU'RE A WINNER
SPECTACULAR JOB
YOU MADE MY DAY
YOU'RE WONDERFUL
YOU ARE EXCITING
YOU'RE IMPORTANT
YOU'RE BEAUTIFUL
I'M PROUD OF YOU
YOU'RE ON TARGET
YOU ARE EXCITING
HIP, HIP, HOORAY
YOU'RE IMPORTANT
YOU'RE FANTASTIC
YOU MAKE ME HAPPY
YOU'RE A TREASURE
BEAUTIFUL SHARING
YOU MAKE ME LAUGH
NOW YOU'RE FLYING
THAT'S INCREDIBLE
YOU'RE GROWING UP
YOU'RE INCREDIBLE
NOW YOU'VE GOT IT

WAY TO BE ON TASK
YOU'RE SENSATIONAL
YOU'RE CATCHING ON
YOU FIGURED IT OUT
THAT'S A GREAT JOB
YOU'RE CATCHING ON
YOU'RE ON YOUR WAY
YOU'RE THE GREATEST
YOU ARE RESPONSIBLE
WHAT AN IMAGINATION
YOU BRIGHTEN MY DAY
YOU'RE ON TOP OF IT
YOU'VE GOT A FRIEND
YOU MEAN A LOT TO ME
YOU'RE DOING SO WELL
YOU LEARNED IT RIGHT
YOU'RE A REAL TROUPER
A BIG HUG / A BIG KISS
I KNEW YOU COULD DO IT
EXCEPTIONAL PERFORMANCE
NOTHING CAN STOP YOU NOW

I LOVE YOU

If your parents never had children, chances are you won't, either.
Dick Cavett

THINGS MY MOTHER TAUGHT ME:
AUTHOR UNKNOWN

My mother taught me LOGIC.
"Because I said so, that's why."

My Mother taught me MEDICINE...
"If you don't stop crossing your eyes, they're going to freeze that way."

My Mother taught me TO THINK AHEAD...
"If you don't pass your spelling test, you'll never get a good job!"

My Mother taught me ESP...
"Put your sweater on; don't you think that I know when you're cold?"

My Mother taught me TO MEET A CHALLENGE...
"What were you thinking? Answer me when I talk to you...Don't talk back to me!"

My Mother taught me HUMOR...
"When that lawn mower cuts off your toes, don't come running to me."

My Mother taught me how to BECOME AN ADULT...
"If you don't eat your vegetables, you'll never grow up.

My mother taught me ABOUT SEX...
"How do you think you got here?"

My mother taught me about GENETICS...
"You are just like your father!"

My mother taught me about my ROOTS...
"Do you think you were born in a barn?"

My mother taught me about the WISDOM of AGE...
"When you get to be my age, you will understand."

My mother taught me about ANTICIPATION...
"Just wait until your father gets home."

My mother taught me about RECEIVING...
"You are going to get it when we get home."

And, my all-time favorite - JUSTICE
"One day you'll have kids, and I hope they turn out just like YOU...then you'll see what it's like."

My mother taught me TO APPRECIATE A JOB WELL DONE.
"If you're going to kill each other, do it outside - I just finished cleaning!"

My mother taught me RELIGION.
"You better pray that will come out of the carpet."

My mother taught me about TIME TRAVEL.
"If you don't straighten up, I'm going to knock you into the middle of next week!"

My mother taught me FORESIGHT.
"Make sure you wear clean underwear, in case you're in an accident."

My mother taught me IRONY.
"Keep laughing and I'll *give* you something to cry about."

My mother taught me about the science of OSMOSIS.
"Shut your mouth and eat your supper!"

My mother taught me about CONTORTIONISM.
"Will you *look* at the dirt on the back of your neck!"

My mother taught me about STAMINA.
"You'll sit there 'til all that spinach is gone."

My mother taught me about WEATHER.
"It looks as if a tornado swept through your room.

My mother taught me how to solve PHYSICS PROBLEMS.
"If I yelled because I saw a meteor coming toward you; would you listen then?"

My mother taught me about HYPOCRISY.
"If I've told you once, I've told you a million times - Don't exaggerate!!!"

My mother taught me THE CIRCLE OF LIFE.
"I brought you into this world, and I can take you out."

My mother taught me about BEHAVIOR MODIFICATION.
"Stop acting like your father!"

My mother taught me about ENVY.
"There are millions of less fortunate children in this world who don't have wonderful parents like you do!"

For rarely are sons similar to their fathers: most are worse, and a few are better than their fathers.
Homer

YOU'VE TURNED INTO A MOM WHEN:

AUTHOR UNKNOWN

- You automatically double-knot everything you tie.
- You find yourself humming the Barney song as you do the dishes.
- You hear a baby cry in the grocery store, and you start to gently sway back and forth, back and forth. However, your children are at school!
- You actually start to like the smell of strained carrots mixed with applesauce.
- You weep through the scene in Dumbo when his mom is taken away, not to mention what Bambi does to you.
- You get soooo into crafts you contemplate writing a book called 101 Fun Crafts to do with Dryer Lint and Eggshells.
- You spend a half hour searching for your sunglasses only to have your teenager say, "Mom, why don't you wear the ones you pushed up on your head?"
- You are out for a nice romantic meal with your husband, enjoying some real adult conversation, when suddenly you realize that you've reached over and started to cut up his steak!

-5-

FRIENDS

One friend in a lifetime is much, two are many, three are hardly possible. Friendship needs a certain parallelism of life, a community of thought, a rivalry of aim.
Henry Brooks Adams

I GIVE TO YOU

AUTHOR UNKNOWN

I Give To You
A fire to light inside your heart,
to feel the warm embers glow.
A piece of the sun's warm rays,
to bask in it's fiery show.

I Give To You
A piece of a rainbow to color your world,
when all seems totally gray.
Some roses for the sweet perfume,
to kiss your senses with its bouquet.

I Give To You
A sprinkling of some twinkling stars,
to wish upon at night.
The morning dew to kiss the day,
To bask in it's delight.

I Give To You
A summer's breeze to caress your face,
to show that someone cares.
The sweet song of the nightingale,
to remind you that I am always there.

I GIVE TO YOU
My lasting friendship, always true.
A gift of love to hold inside,
whenever you feel blue,
or just because you need a friend
This friend...that will always be there for you!!

The friendships of the world are oft confederacies in vice, or leagues of pleasures.
Joseph Addison

THANK YOU

AUTHOR UNKNOWN

Thank you for all the moments we've shared, moments filled with shared dreams and wishes, secrets, laughter, and tears, and above all, friendship. Each precious second will be treasured in my heart forever.

Thank you for taking time, time to stop and take an interest in me; time to listen to my problems and help me find the solutions, and most of all, time to smile at me and show you care..

Thank you for being you you're a wonderful person. You were there when I needed you to confide in and to ask advice from.

Through you, I began to understand and then like myself..
How can I ever tell you how much I care for you??

Thank you my friend...

Friendship is the source of the greatest pleasures, and without friends even the most agreeable pursuits become tedious.
St. Thomas Aquinas

THE GIFT OF FRIENDSHIP

AUTHOR UNKNOWN

Once the package of friendship has been opened,
it can never be closed.
It is a constant book always written...
waiting to be read...and enjoyed.
We may have our disagreements...
we may argue...we may concern one another...
friendship is a unique bond that lasts through it all....
A part of me is put into my friends...
some it is my humor...some it is my listening ear...
some it is real life experiences...
some it is my romanticism...but with all, it is friendship.
Friendships forged are a construct stronger than steel built as a foundation....
necessary for life...and necessary for love.
Friends, you and me.... you brought another friend...
and then there were 3... we started our group...
Our circle of friends... and like that circle...
there is no beginning or end...
FRIENDSHIP IS CONTINOUS

I keep my friends as misers do their treasure, because, of all the things granted us by wisdom, none is greater or better than friendship.

Pietro Aretino

CONFIDE IN A FRIEND

AUTHOR UNKNOWN

When you're tired and worn at the close of day,
And things just don't seem to be going your way.
When even your patience has come to an end, Try taking time out and confide in a friend.

Perhaps she too may have walked the same road,
With a much troubled heart and burdensome load
To find peace and comfort somewhere near the end.
When she stopped long enough to confide in a friend.

For then are most welcome a few words of cheer,
For someone who willingly lends you an ear
No troubles exist that time cannot mend,
But to get quick relief, just confide in a friend.

-6-

LOVE

Never pretend to a love which you do not actually feel, for love is not ours to command.
Alan Watts

SAY IT NOW

AUTHOR UNKNOWN

If you have a tender message,
Or a loving word to say,
Don't wait 'til you forget it,
But whisper it today!

The tender words unspoken,
The letter never sent,
The long-forgotten messages,
The wealth of love unspent...

For these some hearts are breaking,
For these some loved ones wait,
Then give them what they're needing,
Before it is too late!

Love is not enough. It must be the foundation, the cornerstone - but not the complete structure. It is much too pliable, too yielding.
Bette Davis

SHARING
AUTHOR UNKNOWN

A little old couple walked slowly into McDonalds one cold winter evening. They looked out of place amid the young families and young couples eating there that night. Some of the customers looked admiringly at them. You could tell what the admirers were thinking. "Look, there is a couple who has been through a lot together, probably for 60 years or more!"

The little old man walked right up to the cash register, placed his order with no hesitation and then paid for their meal. The couple took a table near the back wall and started taking food off of the tray. There was one hamburger, one order of French fries and one drink.

The little old man unwrapped the plain hamburger and carefully cut it inhalf. He placed one half in front of his wife. Then he carefully counted out the French fries, divided them in two piles and neatly placed one pile in front of his wife. He took a sip of the drink, his wife
took a sip and then set the cup down between them. As the man began to eat his few bites of the hamburger the crowd began to get restless.

Again you could tell what they were thinking. "That poor old couple. All they can afford is one meal for the two of them." As the man began to eat his French fries one young man stood and came over to the old couples' table.

He politely offered to buy another meal for the old couple to eat. The old man replied that they were just fine. They were used to sharing everything. Then the crowd noticed that the little old lady hadn't eaten a bite. She just sat there watching her husband eat and occasionally taking turns sipping the drink.

Again the young man came over and begged them to let him buy them something to eat. This time the lady explained that no, they were used to sharing everything together.

As the little old man finished eating and was wiping his face neatly with a napkin the young man could stand it no longer. Again he came over to their table and offered to buy some food. After being politely refused again he finally asked a question of the little old lady. "Ma'am, why aren't you eating. You said that you share everything. What is it that you are waiting for?"

She answered... "The teeth".

The meeting of two personalities is like the contact of two chemical substances: if there is any reaction, both are transformed.
Carl Jung

HOW GREAT LOVE IS

AUTHOR UNKNOWN

Once upon a time, there was an island where all the feelings lived: Happiness, Sadness, and all of the others including Love.

One day it was announced to the feelings that the island would sink, so all repaired their boats and left. Love was the only one who stayed. Love wanted to persevere until the last possible moment. When the island was almost sinking, Love decided to ask for help.

Richness was passing by Love in a grand boat. Love said, "Richness, can you take me with you?" Richness answered, "No I can't. There is a lot of gold and silver in my boat. There is no place for you here."

Love decided to ask Vanity who was also passing by in a beautiful vessel, "Vanity, please help me!" "I can't help you Love. You are all wet and might damage my boat," Vanity answered.

Sadness was close by so Love asked for help, "Sadness let me go with you." "Oh...Love, I am so sad that I need to be by myself!" Happiness passed by Love too, but she was so happy that she did not even hear when Love called her!

Suddenly, there was a voice, "Come Love, I will take you." It was an elder. Love felt so blessed and overjoyed that he even forgot to ask the elder her name.

When they arrived at dry land, the elder went her own way. Love realizing how much he owed the elder, asked Knowledge, another elder, "Who helped me?"

"It was Time", Knowledge answered. "Time?" asked Love. "But why did Time help me?" Knowledge smiled with deep wisdom and answered, "Because only Time is capable of understanding how great Love is."

To love and be loved is to feel the sun from both sides.
David Viscott

THE PASSENGER

AUTHOR UNKNOWN

The passengers on the bus watched sympathetically as the attractive young woman with the white cane made her way carefully up the steps. She paid the driver and, using her hands to feel the location of the seats, walked down the aisle and found the seat he'd told her was empty. Then she settled in, placed her briefcase on her lap and rested her cane against her leg.

It had been a year since Susan, thirty-four, became blind. Due to a medical misdiagnosis, she had been rendered sightless, and she was suddenly thrown into a world of darkness, anger, frustration and self-pity. Once a fiercely independent woman, Susan now felt condemned by this terrible twist of fate to become a powerless, helpless burden on everyone around her. "How could this have happened to me?" she would plead, her heart knotted with anger. But no matter how much she cried or ranted or prayed, she knew the painful truth-her sight was never going to return. A cloud of depression hung over Susan's once optimistic spirit. Just getting through each day was an exercise in frustration and exhaustion. And all she had to cling to was her husband Mark.

Mark was an Air Force officer, and he loved Susan with all of his heart. When she first lost her sight, he watched her sink into despair and was determined to help his wife gain the strength and confidence she needed to become independent again. Mark's military background had trained him well to deal with sensitive situations, and yet he knew this was the most difficult battle he would ever face.

Finally, Susan felt ready to return to her job, but how would she get there? She used to take the bus, but was now too frightened to get around the city by herself. Mark volunteered to drive her to work each day, even though they worked at opposite ends of the city. At first, this comforted Susan and fulfilled Mark's need to protect his sightless wife who was so insecure about performing the slightest task. Soon, however, Mark realized that this arrangement wasn't working - it was hectic, and costly. Susan is going to have to start taking the bus again, he admitted to himself. But just the thought of mentioning it to her made him cringe. She was still so fragile, so angry. How would she react?

Just as Mark predicted, Susan was horrified at the idea of taking the bus again. "I'm blind!" she responded bitterly. "How am I supposed to know where I'm going? I feel like you're abandoning me." Mark's heart broke to hear these words, but he knew what had to be done. He promised Susan that each morning and evening he would ride the bus with her, for as long as it took, until she got the hang of it. And that is exactly what happened.

For two solid weeks, Mark, military uniform and all, accompanied Susan to and from work each day. He taught her how to rely on her other senses, specifically her hearing, to determine where she was and how to adapt to her new environment. He helped her befriend the bus drivers who could watch out for her, and save her a seat. He made her laugh, even on those not-so-good days when she would trip exiting the bus, or drop her briefcase. Each morning, they made the journey together, and Mark would take a cab back
to his office. Although this routine was even more costly and exhausting than the previous one, Mark knew it was only a matter of time before Susan would be able

to ride the bus on her own. He believed in her, in the Susan he used to know before she'd lost her sight, who wasn't afraid of any challenge and who would never, ever quit. Finally, Susan decided that she was ready to try the trip on her own. Monday morning arrived, and before she left, she threw her arms around Mark, her temporary bus riding companion, her husband, and her best friend. Her eyes filled with tears of gratitude for his loyalty, his patience, his love. She said good-bye, and for the first time, they went their separate ways. Monday, Tuesday, Wednesday, Thursday...Each day on her own went perfectly, and Susan had never felt better. She was doing it! She was going to work all by herself!

On Friday morning, Susan took the bus to work as usual. As she was paying for her fare to exit the bus, the driver said, "Boy, I sure envy you." Susan wasn't sure if the driver was speaking to her or not. After all, who on earth would ever envy a blind woman who had struggled just to find the courage to live for the past year? Curious, she asked the driver, "Why do you say that you envy me?" The driver responded, "It must feel so good to be taken care of and protected like you are." Susan had no idea what the driver was talking about, and asked again, "What do you mean?" The driver answered, "You know, every morning for the past week, a fine looking gentleman in a military uniform has been standing across the corner watching you when you get off the bus. He makes sure you cross the street safely, and he watches you until you enter your office building. Then he blows you a kiss, gives you a little salute and walks away. You are one lucky lady."

Tears of happiness poured down Susan's cheeks. For although she couldn't physically see him, she had always felt Mark's presence. She was blessed, so blessed, for he had given her a gift more powerful than sight, a gift she didn't need to see to believe - the gift of love that can bring light where there had been darkness.

God watches over us in just the same way. We may not know He is present. We may not be able to see His face, but He is there nonetheless!

Oh, life is a glorious cycle of song,
A medley of extemporanea;
And love is a thing that can never go wrong;
And I am Marie of Roumania.
Dorothy Parker

50 WAYS TO SAY "I LOVE YOU"

AUTHOR UNKNOWN

1. Fresh baked cookies and milk says it every time, no matter how old you are.
2. Put a note in their lunch to remind them they are important to you.
3. Go on a date - for no reason!
4. Send flowers to arrive at home when you are out of town on business.
5. Watch The Princess Bride together. Then work "As you wish," into your vocabulary.
6. Do the dishes...without being asked.
7. Give 'em a hug...a good, solid "bear hug"!
8. Keep a journal at home, where anyone can write ideas and thoughts down.
9. Instead of buying a birthday card...make it!
10. Take him or her to a restaurant they love (but, it's not your favorite).
11. The quietest way to say it is to simply listen. No matter who it is, there will be days when you're the only one who does.
12. Meet your child for lunch...in the cafeteria!
13. If you're married, propose again. And again. And again. Find different romantic ways to pop the question.
14. If you're married, propose again. And again. And again. Find different romantic ways to pop the question.
15. Say Thank you.

16. Have dinner and everything ready on the table when they get home.
17. When was the last time you checked your child's homework?
18. Don't forget the classics: breakfast in bed (or even coffee), holding hands, a backrub or foot massage, a nice long hug, opening doors for each other.
19. Kidnap them! Pack an overnight bag for your love, bring a bottle of champagne, and surprise him or her with an overnight at a "fancy" or "fun" place.
20. Take out the trash.
21. Ask how their day was...and listen to the answer.
22. Dig out the old photos and make a scrapbook together.
23. Whenever you've been apart (even for a few hours), make sure he/she knows that you're happy to be together again. "I missed you," is just another way of saying, "I love you".
24. Make a fifteen minute appointment in your calendar to call a family member just to say hi.
25. Take off early (both of you) from work and go to a matinee movie together.
26. Have a little brother or sister? Invite 'em to hang out with you for a night - it won't kill you and they'll think you're so cool!
27. Be spontaneous!
28. Write I LOVE YOU on the mirror with shaving cream before you leave
29. Call your mom or dad and tell them where you are...they do worry about you.
30. Put your kids' artwork on the fridge...it really does make them feel good.
31. Make a standing, monthly date with your mom or dad...just the 2 of you!
32. If you are married, have a second wedding to celebrate your anniversary with minister, church and guests.
33. Learn to say, "I love you" in lots of different languages. Teach them to the person you want to say it to.

34. Volunteer in your child's classroom - even if it's just to cut out 23 paper bears...it shows you care.
35. Take pictures of yourselves kissing in as many places as you can. Put them into a photo album. Give him/her the album.
36. Call your grandparents on Grandparents Day!
37. Stay home and light a fire, eat dinner on the floor and watch an old, classic romantic movie.
38. Buy your child something they love to wear, even though you don't!
39. Create a cocktail or a special dish and name it after him/her.
40. If you're in college, send your mom or dad a letter (snail mail!)...they'll love it!
41. Volunteer to baby-sit your little brother or sister so your parents can go out for the evening.
42. Call and leave a voice mail late one night so that it's the first message he/she gets in the morning.
43. Tell the truth.
44. Pick a room - and clean it up! You'll make someone happy (and you might find that other black sock!).
45. Make his/her passions your passions. Find out what he/she really enjoys doing. Spend time doing it together.
46. Put your hands on their shoulders - look them in the eye - and say, "I'll always love you".
47. Use those "Post-It's"! Leave Hi's and I Love You's all over the place.
48. Laundry - need we say more?
49. Don't take life too seriously - laugh as much as possible.
50. Take time to listen...

When love is in excess it brings a man nor honor nor any worthiness.
Euripides .

PUPPY SIZE

AUTHOR UNKNOWN

"Danielle keeps repeating it over and over again. We've been back to this animal shelter at least five times. It has been weeks now since we started all of this," the mother told the volunteer. "What is it she keeps asking for?" the volunteer asked. "Puppy size!" replied the mother. "Well, we have plenty of puppies, if that's what she's looking for." "I know...we have seen most of them," the mom said in frustration....Just then Danielle came walking into the office. "Well, did you find one?" asked her mom. "No, not this time," Danielle said with sadness in her voice. "Can we come back on the weekend?" The two women looked at each other, shook their heads and laughed "You never know when we will get more dogs. Unfortunately, there's always a supply," the volunteer said. Danielle took her mother by the hand and headed to the door. "Don't worry, I'll find one this weekend," she said.

Over the next few days both mom and dad had long conversations with her. They both felt she was being too particular. "It's this weekend or we're not looking any more," Dad finally said in frustration. "We don't want to hear anything more about puppy size either," Mom added. Sure enough, they were the first ones in the shelter on Saturday morning. By now Danielle knew her way around, so she ran right for the section that housed the smaller dogs. Tired of the routine, mom sat in the small waiting room at the end of the first row of cages. There was an observation window so you could see the animals during times when visitors weren't permitted.

Danielle walked slowly from cage to cage, kneeling periodically to take a closer look. One by
one the dogs were brought out and she held each one. One by one she said, "Sorry, you're not the one."

It was the last cage on this last day in search of the perfect pup. The volunteer opened the cage door and the child carefully picked up the dog and held it closely. This time she took a little longer. "Mom, that's it! I found the right puppy! He's the one! I know it!" she screamed with joy. "It's the puppy size!" "But it's the same size as all the other puppies you held over the last few weeks," Mom said. "No not size ---- the sighs. When I held him in my arms, he sighed," she said. "Don't you remember? When I asked you one day what love is, you told me love depends on the sighs of your heart. The more you love, the bigger the sigh!" The two women looked at each other for a moment. Mom didn't know whether to laugh or cry. As she stooped down to hug the child, she did a little of both.

"Mom, every time you hold me, I sigh. When you and Daddy come home from work and hug each other, you both sigh. I knew I would find the right puppy if it sighed when I held it in my arms," she said. Then holding the puppy up close to her face she said, "Mom, he loves me. I heard the sighs of his heart!"

Close your eyes for a moment and think about the love that makes you sigh. I not only find it in the arms of my loved ones, but in the caress of a sunset, the kiss of the moonlight and the gentle brush of cool air on a hot day. They are the sighs of God. Take the time to stop and listen; you will be surprised at what you hear.

"Life is not measured by the breaths we take, but by the moments that take our breath away."

-7-

HAPPINESS

QUOTES ON HAPPINESS

A person is never happy except at the price of some ignorance.
Anatole France

The discovery of a new dish does more for human happiness than the discovery of a new star.
Anthelme Brillat-Savarin,

Do not weep; do not wax indignant. Understand.
Baruch Spinoza

All sanity depends on this: that is should be a delight to feel heat strike the skin, a delight to stand upright, knowing the bones are moving easily under the flesh.
Doris Lessing

Slow down and enjoy life. It's not only the scenery you miss by going too fast - you also miss the sense of where you are going and why.
Eddie Cantor

A lifetime of happiness! No man alive could bear it: it would be hell on earth.
George Bernard Shaw

Happiness is having a large, loving, caring, close-knit family in another city.
George Burns

To be stupid, selfish, and have good health are three requirements for happiness, though if stupidity is lacking, all is lost.
Gustave Flaubert

Many persons have a wrong idea of what constitutes true happiness. It is not attained through self-gratification but through fidelity to a worthy purpose.
Helen Keller

I am a kind of paranoiac in reverse. I suspect people of plotting to make me happy.
J. D. Salinger

At the height of laughter, the universe is flung into a kaleidoscope of new possibilities.
Jean Houston

Happiness: a good bank account, a good cook and a good digestion.
Jean-Jacques Rousseau

True happiness is of a retired nature, and an enemy to pomp and noise; it arises, in the first place, from the enjoyment of one's self, and in the next from the friendship and conversation of a few select companions.
Joseph Addison

It is pretty hard to tell what does bring happiness; poverty and wealth have both failed.
Kin Hubbard

I've grown to realize the joy that comes from little victories is preferable to the fun that comes from ease and the pursuit of pleasure.
Lawana Blackwell

I cannot believe that the inscrutable universe turns on an axis of suffering; surely the strange beauty of the world must somewhere rest on pure joy!
Louise Bogan

Very little is needed to make a happy life.
Marcus Aurelius Antoninus

When you reliquish the desire to control your future, you can have more happiness.
Nicole Kidman

Happiness isn't something you experience; it's something you remember.
Oscar Levant

One of the keys to happiness is a bad memory.
Rita Mae Brown

Happiness makes up in height for what it lacks in length.
Robert Frost

Remember that happiness is a way of travel - not a destination.
Roy M. Goodman

100 WAYS TO BE A HAPPIER PERSON

AUTHOR UNKNOWN

1) Spend less money than you make.
2) Don't blame other people for your problems.
3) Admit it when you make a mistake.
4) Give all the clothes that you haven't worn in the last three years to charity.
5) Do something nice for someone often and try not to get caught at it.
6) Listen more than you talk.
7) Stop thinking you need to have a strong opinion about everything.
8) Invite a university student to eat lunch at your home periodically.
9) Take a thirty-minute walk or run every day.
10 Skip two meals a week and give the money to the hungry or the homeless.
11) Have a daily devotional.
12) Attend Sunday school and worship every Sunday.
13) Be on time.
14) Don't make excuses.
15) Be kind to the kind and to the unkind.
16) Get organized.
17) Spend time with your family.
18) Don't argue.
19) Read good books.
20) Read a newspaper daily and a newsmagazine weekly.
21) Strive for excellence, not for perfection.
22) Cultivate good manners.
23) Don't be critical of other people.
24) Take your responsibilities seriously but not yourself seriously.
25) Don't get set in your ways.

26) Learn something new every day.
27) Have at least four friends with which you maintain contact.
28) Live in the present but plan for the future.
29) Maintain your property and possessions.
30) Don't sweat the small stuff.
31) Watch your diet and your weight.
32) Be as gracious to other people as you want God to be to you.
33) Live by these three priorities: God, others, and self.
34) Practice recycling and ecology.
35) Don't be envious or jealous.
36) Count your blessings often.
37) Finish what you start.
38) Have short term, long term, and lifetime goals.
39) Learn to say the four magic words of success: I need your help.
40) Listen to good music.
41) Watch less television.
42) Take vitamins.
43) Develop a hobby.
44) Participate in a sport.
45) Reduce the obligation that diminishes you spiritually and emotionally.
46) Be generous with your money.
47) Mind your own business.
48) Stop thinking you have to own everything you enjoy.
49) Keep a daily journal of your thoughts, prayers and dreams.
50) Give some time every week to solving a problem in the community that concerns you.
51) Get eight hours sleep per night.
52) Do more work than your employer can reasonably expect.

53) Take a day off each quarter and a vacation each year.
54) Have an exercise program.
55) Grow something.
56) Keep up to date with your correspondence.
57) Be kind to animals.
58) Do only one thing at a time.
59) Never get out of touch with young people.
60) Show respect for your elders.
61) Have a date with your mate once a week.
62) Be aware of how vulnerable you are to bad habits and addictions.
63) Get up early in the morning.
64) Make the best of your circumstances.
65) Don't try to please everybody.
66) Work smarter not harder.
67) Be the best you can be at whatever task is set before you.
68) Know your strengths and your weaknesses.
69) Say "please," "thank you", "sir," and "ma'am" a lot.
70) Laugh and smile a lot.
71) Never betray confidences.
72) Compliment someone every day.
73) Vote.
74) Write your elected representatives from time to time.
75) Keep your will up to date.
76) Sign a living will and an organ donor card.
77) Keep your promises.
78) Never lie, cheat, or steal.
79) Remember people's names.
80) Don't procrastinate.

81) Praise in public and criticize in private.
82) Tell your loved ones you love them often.
83) Don't discuss salary, property, debts, or net worth.
84) Buy the best shoes, chair and bed that money can buy.
85) Don't gossip or repeat gossip.
86) Learn to appreciate good art.
87) Always have something to which you are looking forward.
88) Maintain control of your sexual urges.
89) Forgive others and yourself.
90) Spend time periodically in silence and solitude.
91) Be yourself even if it means you are different from others.
92) Never use profanity.
93) Learn CPR.
94) Turn off the television, radio, and telephone during meals.
95) Have regular physical and dental checkups.
96) Avoid negative people.
97) Read the fine print.
98) Drive the speed limit.
99) Drink a lot of water.
100) Make up your mind to be happy.

100 Ways to Be Happy and Feel Good!

AUTHOR UNKNOWN

1. Never put yourself last.
2. When you extend a helping hand to one person, be careful not to let go of the other.
3. Always own a pair of old, faded jeans.
4. Count your blessings every day.
5. Acknowledge your successes along with your downfalls.
6. Burn the candle that has been in storage for the last two years.
7. Strive for progress, not perfection.
8. Remember, the voice telling you that you cannot do something is always lying.
9. At least once a day sit and do nothing.
10. Don't close your heart so tightly against life's pain that you shut out life's blessings.
11. Celebrate all your birthdays no matter how old you get.
12. Examine your life for limitations and ask yourself why you put hem there.
13. Plant a tree, pull weeds, or get your hands dirty.
14. Diminish your wants instead of increasing your needs.
15. Cry when you feel like it.
16. Rejoice in other people's triumphs.
17. Don't wait for someone else to laugh or express joy.
18. Forgive yourself for any mistake you make, no matter how big or small.
19. Keep good company.
20. Never take a pill for a pain you need to feel.
21. Use your enthusiasm to put yourself in forward gear and give yourself a spark to move ahead.
22. Look in the eyes of the ones you love when you are talking to them.

23. Remember that one is a whole number.
24. Walk in a summer rain shower without an umbrella.
25. Do a kind deed for someone else.
26. Keep your eyes and ears open to get the messages you need from people and events in your daily life.
27. Be patient.
28. Eat something green.
29. Change what you can and leave the rest alone.
30. Walk hand and hand with truth.
31. Make laughter and joy a greater part of your life than anger and grief.
32. Embrace solitude instead of running from it.
33. Be zealous, not jealous.
34. Forgive anyone you've been holding a grudge against.
35. Slow down and enjoy the present.
36. Walk in others' shoes before judging them.
37. Send yourself a kind message.
38. Remind yourself that the company you keep is a reflection of what you think of yourself.
39. Go on a picnic.
40. Accept your fears, no matter how crazy they seem.
41. Don't let other people's opinions shape who you are.
42. Say a prayer.
43. Never attribute your accomplishments to luck or chance.
44. Know when to say no.
45. Look at the positive side of negative situation.
46. Remember that you are a spiritual being in a physical body.
47. Avoid seeking out other people for constant approval, because it make them the master and you the slave.

48. Go fly a kite.
49. Avoid fads and bandwagons.
50. Accept the things you cannot change.
51. Look inside instead of outside yourself for answers to life's problems.
52. Remember that all feelings are okay.
53. Shield yourself from bad influences.
54. Stand up for what you believe in.
55. Respect the wishes of others when they say no.
56. Seize every moment and live it fully.
57. Give away or sell anything you haven't used in the past five years .
58. Never downgrade yourself.
59. Take responsibility for what you think, feel, and do.
60. Pamper yourself.
61. Never say or do anything abusive to a child.
62. Let yourself be God powered instead of flying solo.
63. Volunteer to help someone in need.
64. Refrain from overindulging in food, drink, and work
65. Finish unfinished business.
66. Be spontaneous.
67. Find a constructive outlet for your anger.
68. Think about abundance instead of lack, because whatever you think about expands.
69. Think of yourself as a survivor, not a victim.
70. Cuddle an animal.
71. Be open to life.
72. See success as something you already have, not something you must attain.
73. Experience the splendor and awe of a sunset.
74. When you score a base hit, don't wish it were a home run.

75. Learn to be in the present moment.
76. Instead of believing in miracles, depend on them.
77. Take a child to the circus.
78. Change your attitude and your whole life will change.
79. Never turn your power over to another person.
80. When your heart is at odds with your head, follow your heart.
81. Always remember that the past is gone forever and the future never comes.
82. Live your life according to what is right for you.
83. Acknowledge your imperfections.
84. Plant a tree and watch it grow.
85. See "friend" instead of "enemy" on the face of strangers.
86. Watch an army of ants build their houses and cities and carry food ten times their weight.
87. Believe in something bigger than yourself.
88. Let the playful child within you come out.
89. Make haste slowly.
90. Work through your problems step by step and one day at a time.
91. Accept compliments from others so you can see the truth about yourself.
92. Sit on the lawn without worrying about grass stains.
93. Don't condemn yourself for your imperfections.
94. Do a humility check periodically by loving the truth about yourself.
95. Tell someone you appreciate them.
96. Never live your life according to what is right for someone else.
97. Talk less and listen more.
98. Admit your wrongdoing and forgive yourself for it.
99. Thrive on inner peace instead of on crises.
100. Affirm all the good things about yourself.

-8-

DREAMS

QUOTES ON DREAMS

I know how men in exile feed on dreams of hope
Aeschylus

Dreams that do come true can be as unsettling as those that don't.
Brett Butler

He felt that his whole life was some kind of dream and he sometimes wondered whose it was and whether they were enjoying it.
Douglas Adams

Dreams surely are difficult, confusing, and not everything in them is brought to pass for mankind. For fleeting dreams have two gates: one is fashioned of horn and one of ivory. Those which pass through the one of sawn ivory are deceptive, bringing tidings which come to nought, but those which issue from the one of polished horn bring true results when a mortal sees them.
Homer

Keep true to the dreams of thy youth.
Johann von Schiller

Now, I say to you today my friends, even though we face the difficulties of today and tomorrow, I still have a dream. It is a dream deeply rooted in the American dream. I have a dream that one day this nation will rise up and live out the true meaning of its creed: - 'We hold these truths to be self-evident, that all men are created equal.'
Martin Luther King Jr.

Last night I dreamed I ate a ten-pound marshmallow, and when I woke up the pillow was gone.
Tommy Cooper

There is nothing like dream to create the future. Utopia to-day, flesh and blood tomorrow.
Victor Hugo

Dreaming permits each and every one of us to be quietly and safely insane every night of our lives.
William Dement

There are more things in heaven and earth, Horatio, Than are dreamt of in your philosophy.
William Shakespeare

What if nothing exists and we're all in somebody's dream? Or what's worse, what if only that fat guy in the third row exists?
Woody Allen

DREAMS

AUTHOR UNKNOWN

When we were young, we had dreams and expectations. We imagine things, we keep thinking about what we want to be, what we want to do, what makes us proud and happy and what will we become.

We grew up, and things seemed like having its own way. We accept our success or failures and we move on. The rapid change, the need to do the urgent things, the works, the pressures and the failures, all kill part of our visions.

Things have changed, but they cannot really take away the dreams. We still have to dream on, to visualize our desires, our wants, our vision of our future, even when we are considered too old for such things.

Colonel Sanders started his business when he was sixty, and started the whole successful KFC business. The main thing is not the age - whether being too old, or too young, but it is the desire to dream on, and the courage to realize it.

Vivid visualization, taking it to sleep, thinking constantly about it, talking about it, planning it, adding all the spices to our dreams will make us a bit closer to the realization of our dreams.

Entrepreneurship starts with a dream, a simple wish of tiny restaurant operation, or a huge business of real-estate development, or a modest training center for English education, or just any other self-employed money earning fun.

The ability to dream on is one of the fine quality of human race that other species do not possess. So dream on, and put a deadline: make it a giant dream, a tiny one, an old everlasting one, a newfound one, a hobby related one, a change of life one, a religious one, a stupid one, a stroke-of-genius one, or just whatever...... just continue to dream on........ Then, Just Go and Do It!

GROW GREAT BY DREAMS

AUTHOR UNKNOWN

The question was once asked of a highly successful businessman: "How have you done so much in your lifetime?"

He replied, "I have dreamed. I have turned my mind loose to imagine what I wanted to do. Then I have gone to bed and thought about my dreams. In the night I dreamt about my dreams. And when I awoke in the morning, I saw the way to make my dreams real. While other people were saying, 'You can't do that, it isn't possible,' I was well on my way to achieving what I wanted." As Woodrow Wilson, 28th President of the U.S., said: "We grow great by dreams. All big men are dreamers."

They see things in the soft haze of a spring day, or in the red fire on a long winter's evening. Some of us let these great dreams die, but others nourish and protect them; nourish them through bad days until they bring them to the sunshine and light which comes always to those who sincerely hope that their dreams will come true."

So please, don't let anyone steal your dreams, or try to tell you they are too impossible.
"Sing your song, dream your dreams, hope your hope and pray your prayer."

-9-

WORK & SUCCESS

QUOTES ON WORK

Man is so made that he can only find relaxation from one kind of labor by taking up another.
Anatole France

Opportunities are usually disguised as hard work, so most people don't recognize them.
Ann Landers

All paid jobs absorb and degrade the mind.
Aristotle

One of the symptoms of an approaching nervous breakdown is the belief that one's work is terribly important.
Bertrand Russell

It has been my experience that one cannot, in any shape or form, depend on human relations for lasting reward. It is only work that truly satisfies.
Bette Davis

Hard work never killed anybody, but why take a chance?
Charlie McCarthy

When a man tells you that he got rich through hard work, ask him: 'Whose?'
Don Marquis

A human being must have occupation if he or she is not to become a nuisance to the world.
Dorothy L. Sayers

Get happiness out of your work or you may never know what happiness is.
Elbert Hubbard

Measure not the work until the day's out and the labor done.
Elizabeth Barrett Browning

Derive happiness in oneself from a good day's work, from illuminating the fog that surrounds us.
Henri Matisse

Work while you have the light. You are responsible for the talent that has been entrusted to you.
Henri-Frédéric Amiel

Do not hire a man who does your work for money, but him who does it for love of it.
Henry David Thoreau

When your work speaks for itself, don't interrupt.
Henry J. Kaiser

Life grants nothing to us mortals without hard work.
Horace

...in order that a man may be happy, it is necessary that he should not only be capable of his work, but a good judge of his work.
John Ruskin

In order that people may be happy in their work, these three things are needed: They must be fit for it: They must not do too much of it: And they must have a sense of success in it.
John Ruskin

Never continue in a job you don't enjoy. If you're happy in what you're doing, you'll like yourself, you'll have inner peace. And if you have that, along with physical health, you will have had more success than you could possibly have imagined.
Johnny Carson

My work is a game, a very serious game.
M. C. Escher

The sweat of hard work is not to be displayed. It is much more graceful to appear favored by the gods.
Maxine Hong Kingston, The Woman Warrior, 1976

People who work sitting down get paid more than people who work standing up.
Ogden Nash

Anyone can do any amount of work provided it isn't the work he is supposed to be doing at the moment.
Robert Benchley

FROM "ACTUAL" PERFORMANCE EVALUATIONS!

AUTHOR UNKNOWN

These individual quotes were reportedly taken from actual employee performance evaluations throughout the U.S. Hopefully, none of us will be seeing similar ones on ours.

• Since my last report, this employee has reached rock bottom and has started to dig.

• His men would follow him anywhere, but only out of curiosity.

• I would not allow this employee to breed.

• This employee is really not so much of a has-been, but more of a definite won't be.

• Works well when under constant supervision and cornered like a rat in a trap.

• When she opens her mouth, it seems that it is only to change feet.

• He would be out of his depth in a parking lot puddle.

• This young lady has delusions of adequacy.

• He sets low personal standards and then consistently fails to achieve them.
• This employee is depriving a village somewhere of an idiot.

- This employee should go far, and the sooner he starts, the better.
- He's got a full 6-pack, but lacks the plastic thing to hold it all together.
- A gross ignoramus - - - 144 times worse than an ordinary ignoramus.
- He certainly takes a long time to make his pointless.
- He doesn't have ulcers, but he's a carrier.
- I would like to go hunting with him sometime.
- He's been working with glue too much.
- He would argue with a signpost.
- He has a knack for making strangers immediately.
- He brings a lot of joy whenever he leaves the room.
- When his IQ reaches 50, he should sell.
- If you see two people talking, and one looks bored, he's the other one.
- A photographic memory but with the lens cover glued on.
- A prime candidate for Natural de-Selection.

- Donated his brain to science before he was done using it.
- Gates are down, lights are flashing, but the train isn't coming.
- Has two brains: one is lost and the other is out looking for it.
- If he were any more stupid, he'd have to be watered twice a week.
- If you gave him a penny for his thoughts, you'd get change.
- If you stand close enough to him, you can hear the oceans.
- It's hard to believe that he beat out 1,000,000 other sperm.
- One neuron short of a Synapse.
- Some drink from the fountain of knowledge, he only gargled.
- Takes him 1.5 hours to watch 60 Minutes.
- The wheel is still turning, but the hamster is dead.

I LOVE MY JOB!
THE LOST DR SEUSS POEM
AUTHOR UNKNOWN

I love my job, I love the pay!
I love it more and more each day.
I love my boss, she is the best!
I love her boss and all the rest.

I love my office and its location,
I hate to have to go on vacation.
I love my furniture, drab and gray,
And piles of paper that grow each day!

I think my job is really swell,
There's nothing else I love so well.
I love to work among my peers,
I love their leers, and jeers, and sneers.

I love my computer and its software;
I hug it often though it won't care.
I love each program and every file.
I'd love them more if they worked a while.

I'm happy to be here. I am. I am.
I'm the happiest slave of the Firm, I am.
I love this work, I love these chores.
I love the meetings with deadly bores.

I love my job - I'll say it again -
I even love those friendly men.
Those friendly men who've come today,
In clean white coats to take me away!

TOP 10 SIGNS OF JOB BURN OUT

AUTHOR UNKNOWN

10. You're so tired, you now answer the phone with just: "Hell."

9. Your friends call to ask how you've been, and you immediately scream, "Get off my back!!"

8. Your garbage can IS your "In" box.

7. You wake up to discover your bed is on fire, but go back to sleep because you just don't care.

6. You have so much on your mind, you've forgotten how to LOGON.

5. Visions of the upcoming weekend help you make it through Monday.

4. You don't set your alarm anymore because you know the pager will go off before the alarm does.

3. You leave for a party and instinctively bring your ID badge.

2. Your DayTimer/Work Planner exploded a week ago.

And the number one sign that you are burned out because of work?
1. You think about how relaxing it would be if you were in jail right now

QUOTES ON SUCCESS

If at first you don't succeed; you are running about average.
M. H. Alderson

You are wholly complete and your success in life will be in direct proportion to your ability to accept this truth about you.
Dr. Robert Anthony

Success, or failure, very often arrives on wings that seem mysterious to us.
Dr. Marcus Bach

Many a man owes his success to his first wife and his second wife to his success.
Jim Backus

Character is more important than intelligence for success.
Gilberte Beaux

Ones best success comes after their greatest disappointments.
Henry Ward Beecher

The measure of a man's success must be according to his ability. The advancement he makes from the station in which he was born gives the degree of his success.
Sir Walter Besant

A young person, to achieve, must first get out of his mind any notion either of the ease or rapidity of success. Nothing ever just happens in this world.
Edward William Bok

Behind every successful man there's a lot of unsuccessful years.
Bob Brown

The person who tries to live alone will not succeed as a human being. His heart withers if it does not answer another heart. His mind shrinks away if he hears only the echoes of his own thoughts and finds no other inspiration.
Pearl S. Buck

Success is important only to the extent that it puts one in a position to do more things one likes to do.
Sarah Caldwell

It takes twenty years to become an overnight success.
Eddie Cantor

The person who goes farthest is generally the one who is willing to do and dare. The sure-thing boat never gets far from shore.
Dale Carnegie

Success is the sum of small efforts, repeated day in and day out...
Robert Collier

To know a man, observe how he wins his object, rather than how he loses it; for when we fail, our pride supports; when we succeed; it betrays us.
Charles Caleb Colton

It's the men behind who "make" the man ahead.
Merle Crowell

Success is not something I've wrapped my brain around. If people go to those movies, then yes, that's true, big-time success. If not, it's much ado about nothing. [On the prospects for his 1997 movies The Rainmaker and Good Will Hunting]
Matt Damon

The road to success runs uphill.
Willie Davis

To succeed means that you may have to step out of line and march to the sound of your own drummer.
Keith Degreen

Success is counted sweetest by those who never succeed.
Emily Dickinson

I do not like to repeat successes, I like to go on to other things.
Walt Disney

Every man has a right to be conceited until he is successful.
Benjamin Disraeli

SUCCESS:

AUTHOR UNKNOWN

At age 4 success is . . . not wetting your pants.
At age 12 success is . . . having friends.
At age 16 success is . . . having a drivers license.
At age 20 success is . . . having sex.
At age 35 success is . . . having money.
At age 50 success is . . . having money.
At age 60 success is . . . having sex.
At age 70 success is . . . having a drivers license.
At age 75 success is . . . having friends.
At age 80 success is . . . not wetting your pants.

COMFORT ZONE

AUTHOR UNKNOWN

I use to have a Comfort Zone
Where I knew I couldn't fail
The same four walls of busy work
Were really more like jail.

I longed so much to do the things
I'd never done before,
But I stayed inside my Comfort Zone
And paced the same old floor

I said it didn't matter,
That I wasn't doing much
I said I didn't care for things
Like diamonds, furs and such

I claimed to be so busy
With the things inside my zone,
But deep inside I longed for
Something special of my own.

I couldn't let my life go by,
Just watching others win.
I held my breath and stepped outside
And let the change begin.

I took a step and with new strength
I'd never felt before,
I kissed my Comfort Zone "goodbye"
And closed and locked the door.

If you are in a Comfort Zone,
Afraid to venture out,
Remember that all winners were
At one time filled with doubt.

A step or two and words of praise,
Can make your dreams come true.
Greet your future with a smile,
Success is there for you!

-10-

SPIRITUALITY

QUOTES ON SPIRITUALITY

Don't you believe that there is in man a deep so profound as to be hidden even to him in whom it is?
St. Augustine

The spiritual is the parent of the practical.
Thomas Carlyle

Be free all worthy spirits, and stretch yourselves, for greatness and for height.
George Champman

I'm aware that people I have loved and have died and are in the spirit world look after me.
Princess of Wales Diana

What I am trying to do is to unmuddle the metaphysical.
Wayne Dyer

The foundations of a person are not in matter but in spirit.
Ralph Waldo Emerson

All earthly delights are sweeter in expectation than in enjoyment; but all spiritual pleasures more in fruition than in expectation.
Francois FéNelon

The man or woman who concentrated on "Things" can hardly be trusted to use those things for the essential good of mankind. Only those who have guided the development of their spirit as well as their mind are really; qualified to use wisely the things that man's reason has enabled him to fashion out of nature's raw materials.
E. S. Fields

His spiritual life has been exaggerated by a chronic attack of mental gallstones.
Oliver St. John Gogarty

Ghost only exist for those who wish to see them.
Holtei

Your treasure house is within; it contains all you'll ever need.
Hui-Hai

The sensual and spiritual are linked together by a mysterious bond, sensed by our emotions, though hidden from our eyes. To this double nature of the visible and invisible world -- to the profound longing for the latter, coupled with the feeling of the sweet necessity for the former, we owe all sound and logical systems of philosophy, truly based on the immutable principles of our nature, just as from the same source arise the most senseless enthusiasms.
Karl Wilhelm Von Humboldt

Pure Spirit, one hundred degrees proof -- that's a drink that only the most hardened contemplation-guzzlers indulge in. Bodhisattvas dilute their Nirvana with equal parts of love and work.
Aldous Huxley

Spirit is matter seen in a stronger light.
L. P. Jacks

He who interrupts the course of his spiritual exercises and prayer is like a man who allows a bird to escape from his hand; he can hardly catch it again.
St. John of the Cross

There is no easy formula for determining right and wrong livelihood, but it is essential to keep the question alive. To return the sense of dignity and honor to manhood, we have to stop pretending that we can make a living at something that is trivial or destructive and still have sense of legitimate self-worth. A society in which vocation and job are separated for most people gradually creates an economy that is often devoid of spirit, one that frequently fills our pocketbooks at the cost of emptying our souls.
Sam Keen

As long as I can remember I feel I have had this great creative and spiritual force within me that is greater than faith, greater than ambition, greater than confidence, greater than determination, greater than vision. It is all these combined. My brain becomes magnetized with this dominating force which I hold in my hand.
Bruce Lee

Whether we name divine presence synchronicity, serendipity, or graced moment matters little. What matters is the reality that our hearts have been understood. Nothing is as real as a healthy dose of magic which restores our spirits.
Nancy Long

It must be of the spirit if we are to save the flesh.
Douglas Macarthur

Under all that we think, lives all we believe, like the ultimate veil of our spirits.
Antonio Machado

At the center of our being is a point of nothingness which is untouched by sin and by illusion, a point of pure truth, a point or spark which belongs entirely to God, which is never at our disposal, from which God disposes of our lives, which is inaccessible to the fantasies of our own mind or the brutalities of our own will.
Thomas Merton

Once spirit was God, then it became man, and now it is even becoming mob.
Friedrich Nietzsche

Spiritual power begins by directing animal power to other than egoistic ends.
John Ruskin

Physical strength is measured by what we can carry; spiritual by what we can bear.
Source Unknown

THE LORD'S QUIZ
AUTHOR UNKNOWN

One day a while back, a man, his heart heavy with grief, was walking in the woods. As he thought about his life this day, he knew many things were not right. He thought about those who had lied about him back when he had a job. His thoughts turned to those who had stolen his things and cheated him. He remembered family that had passed on. His mind turned to the illness he had that no one could cure. His very soul was filled with anger, resentment and frustration. Standing there this day, searching for answers he could not find, knowing all else had failed him, he knelt at the base of an old oak tree to seek the one he knew would always be there. And with tears in his eyes, he prayed: "Lord- You have done wonderful things for me in this life. You have told me to do many things for you, and I happily obeyed. Today, you have told me to forgive. I am sad, Lord, because I cannot. I don't know how. It is not fair Lord. I didn't deserve these wrongs that were done against me and I shouldn't have to forgive. As perfect as your way is Lord, this one thing I cannot do, for I don't know how to forgive. My anger is so deep Lord, I fear I may not hear you, but I pray that you teach me to do this one thing I cannot do - Teach me To Forgive."

As he knelt there in the quiet shade of that old oak tree, he felt something fall onto his shoulder. He opened his eyes. Out of the corner of one eye, he saw something red on his shirt. He could not turn to see what it was because where the oak tree had been was a large square piece of wood in the ground. He raised his head and saw two feet held to the wood with a large spike through them.

He raised his head more, and tears came to his eyes as he saw Jesus hanging on a cross. He saw spikes in His hands, a gash in His side, a torn and battered body, deep thorns sunk into His head. Finally he saw the suffering and pain on His precious face. As their eyes met, the man's tears turned to sobbing, and Jesus began to speak.

Have you ever told a lie, he asked? The man answered - yes Lord. Have you ever been given too much change and kept it? The man answered yes Lord. And the man sobbed more and more. Have you ever taken something from work that wasn't yours, Jesus asked?

And the man answered yes Lord.

Have you ever sworn, using my Father's name in vain? The man, crying now, answered yes Lord. As Jesus asked many more times, "Have you ever"? The man's crying became uncontrollable, for he could only answer yes Lord. Then Jesus turned His head from one side to the other, and the man felt something fall on his other shoulder. He looked and saw that it was the blood of Jesus. When he looked back up, his eyes met those of Jesus, and there was a look of love the man had never seen or known before.

Jesus said, I didn't deserve this either, but I forgive you.

It may be hard to see how you're going to get through something, but when you look back in life, you realize how true this statement is.

Read the first line slowly and let it sink in. This is simple, and important. Read on....This first line is deep.

If God brings you to it - He will bring you through it. Lord I love You and I need You, come into my heart, today. For without You I can do nothing.

-11-

GROWING OLDER

CONGRATULATIONS! YOU'VE MADE IT!

AUTHOR UNKNOWN

According to today's regulators and bureaucrats, those of us who were kids in the 40's, 50's, 60's, and 70's probably shouldn't have survived.

Our baby cribs were covered with bright colored lead-based paint. We had no childproof lids on medicine bottles, doors or cabinets, and when we rode our bikes, we had no helmets. Not to mention the risks we took hitchhiking.

As children, we would ride in cars with no seat belts or air bags. Riding in the back of a pickup truck on a warm day was always a special treat.

We drank water from the garden hose and not from a bottle. Horrors!

We ate cupcakes, bread and butter, and drank soda pop with sugar in it, but we were never overweight because we were always outside playing.

We shared one soft drink with four friends, from one bottle, and no one actually died from this.

We would spend hours building our go-carts out of scraps and then rode down the hill, only to find out we forgot the brakes. After running into the bushes a few times, we learned to solve the problem.

We would leave home in the morning and play all day, as long as we were back when the street lights came on.

No one was able to reach us all day. No cell phones. Unthinkable! We did not have Playstations, Nintendo 64, X-Boxes, no video games at all, no 99 channels on cable, video tape movies, surround sound, personal cell phones, personal computers, or Internet chat rooms.

We had friends! We went outside and found them.

We played dodge ball, and sometimes, the ball would really hurt. We fell out of trees, got cut and broke bones and teeth, and there were no lawsuits from these accidents. They were accidents. No one was to blame but us. Remember accidents?

We had fights and punched each other and got black and blue and learned to get over it.

We made up games with sticks and tennis balls and ate worms, and although we were told it would happen, we did not put out very many eyes, nor did the worms live inside us forever.

We rode bikes or walked to a friend's home and knocked on the door, or rang the bell or just walked in and talked to them.

Little League and cheerleaders had tryouts and not everyone made the team. Those who didn't had to learn to deal with disappointment.

Some students weren't as smart as others, so they failed a grade and were held back to repeat the same grade. Horrors!
Tests were not adjusted for any reason.

Our actions were our own. Consequences were expected. The idea of a parent bailing us out if we broke a law was unheard of. They actually sided with the law. Imagine that!

This generation has produced some of the best risk-takers and problem solvers and inventors, ever. The past 50 years have been an explosion of innovation and new ideas. We had freedom, failure, success and responsibility, and we learned how to deal with it all.

And you're one of them! Congratulations.

GRANT ME THE SENILITY
AUTHOR UNKNOWN

God grant me the Senility to forget the people I never liked anyway, the good fortune to run into the ones I do, and the eyesight to tell the difference.

Now that I am older, here's what I have discovered:

I started out with nothing,
& I still have most of it.

My wild oats have turned into
prunes and All Bran.

I finally got my head together,
now my body is falling apart.

Funny, I don't remember being
absent minded...

All reports are in;
Life is now officially unfair.

If all is not lost,
where is it?

Kids in the back seat
cause accidents.

Accidents in the back seat
...cause kids!

It is easier to get older
than it is to get wiser.

Some days you're the dog;
some days you're the hydrant.

I wish the buck stopped here;
I sure could use a few...

It's hard to make a comeback
when you haven't been anywhere.

The only time the world beats a path to your door is when you're in the bathroom.

If God wanted me to touch my toes,
he would have put them on my knees.

When I'm finally holding all the cards,
why does everyone decide to play chess?

It's not hard to meet expenses...
they're everywhere.

The only difference between a rut
and a grave is the depth.

These days I spend a lot of time thinking
about the hereafter...

I go somewhere to get something
& then wonder what I'm here after!

EVERYTHING I NEED TO KNOW, I LEARNED FROM THE EASTER BUNNY

AUTHOR UNKNOWN

Don't put all your eggs in one basket

The best things in life are still sweet and gooey

Walk softly and carry a big carrot

Good things come in small sugarcoated packages

Everyone needs a friend who is all ears

There's no such thing as too much candy

Keep your paws off other people's jelly beans

Everyone is entitled to a bad hare day

All work and no play can make you a basket case

A cute little tail attracts a lot of attention

The grass is always greener in someone else's basket

An Easter bonnet can tame even the wildest hare

To show your true colors you have to come out of your shell

Some body parts should be floppy

Let happy thoughts multiply like rabbits

ODE TO THE OLD

AUTHOR UNKNOWN

Just a line to say I'm living
and that I'm not among the dead
Tho I'm getting more forgetful
and more mixed up in the head

But sometime I can't remember
when I stand at the foot of the stairs
if I must go up for something
or if I've just come down from there-

And before the fridge so often
my poor mind is full of doubt
have I just put food away
or have I come to take it out

And there are times when it's dark out
with my night cap on my head
I don't know if I'm retiring
or just getting out of bed

So if it's my turn to write you
there's no need in getting sore
I may think that I've written you
and don't want to be a bore

Remember that I do love you,
and I wish you were here,
and it's nearly my mail time
so I'll say "goodbye" dear

There I stood beside the mailbox
with my face so very red
instead of mailing you this letter
I've opened it instead-

-12-

THE LIGHTER SIDE OF LIFE

AIRLINE HUMOR

AUTHOR UNKNOWN

After every flight, all pilots complete a gripe sheet which is meant to list problems encountered with the aircraft during the flight.

The mechanics use this checklist to make repair and/or corrections. The actual form is a piece of paper that the pilot completes, and submits to the mechanics for action.

The mechanic must respond...in writing, on the lower half of the form...regarding what was done to the aircraft. The pilot reviews the gripe sheets before the aircraft is put back in service.

Never let it be said that ground crews and engineers are lacking for a sense of humor.

The following are actual logged maintenance complaints and problems, as submitted by QANTAS pilots, along with the solutions recorded by the maintenance engineers.

By the way, QANTAS is the only major airline that has never had a fatal accident.

P = The problem logged by the pilot.
S = The solution and action taken by the engineers.

P: Left inside main tire almost needs replacement.
S: Almost replaced left inside main tire.

P: Test flight OK, except autoland very rough.
S: Autoland not installed on this aircraft.

P: Something loose in cockpit.
S: Something tightened in cockpit.

P: Dead bugs on windshield.
S: Live bugs are currently on backorder.

P: Autopilot in altitude-hold mode produces a 200 fpm (feet per minute) descent.
S: Cannot reproduce problem on ground.

P: Evidence of leak on right main landing gear.
S: Evidence removed.

P: DME volume unbelievably loud.
S: DME volume set to more believable level.

P: Friction locks cause throttle levers to stick.
S: That's what they're there for.

P: IFF inoperative.
S: IFF always inoperative in OFF mode.

P: Suspected crack in windshield.
S: Suspect you're right.

P: Number 3 engine missing.
S: Engine found on right wing after brief search.

P: Aircraft handles funny.
S: Aircraft warned to straighten up, fly right, and be serious.
P: Target radar hums.
S: Reprogrammed target radar with all the words.

P: Mouse in cockpit.
S: Cat installed.

100 WAYS TO BE ANNOYING

AUTHOR UNKNOWN

1- Adjust the tint on your TV so that all the people are green and insist that you "like it that way".

2- Drum on every available surface.

3- When walking through the parking lot re-adjust everybody's rear view mirrors.

4- Sing the "na-na-na-na-na-na-na-na Batman" song incessantly.

5- Staple papers in the middle of the page.

6- Ask 1-800 operators for dates.

7- Produce a rental video consisting entirely of dire FBI copy infringement warnings.

8- Drop anti-theft detectors in peoples pockets as they leave stores.

9- Write the surprise ending to a novel on it's first page.

10- Specify that your drive-through order is "to go."

11- Put dairy products places where they won't be found until well after the expiration date.

12- Set alarms for random times.

13- Learn Morse code and have conversations with friends in public consisting of “Beeep bip bip beeep bip...."

14- Order a side of pork rinds with your fillet mignon.

15- Serve Night Train next Thanksgiving.

16- Flick water at friends' pets.

17- Publicly investigate how slowly you can make a "croaking" noise.

18- Honk your horn all through any red light.

19- Dress only on clothes colored Hunter's Orange.

20- Change channels five minutes before the end of every show.

21- Tape pieces of "Sweating to the Oldies" over climatic parts of rental movies.

22- Begin all of your sentences with "Ooh la la!"

23- Decline to be seated at a restaurant and simply eat their complimentary mints.

24- Leave someone's printer in compressed-italic-cyrillic-landscape mode.

25- Intentionally clog the toilets at parties.

26- Wipe your nose on other peoples' sleeves.

27- Buy a large quantity of orange traffic cones and reroute whole streets.

28- Pay for your dinner with pennies.

29- Tie jingle bells on all of your clothing.

30- Repeat everything someone says, as a question.

31- Write "X-BURIED TREASURE" in random spots on all of somebone's roadmaps.

32- Mix-up kosher silverware and claim ignorance EVERY time.

33- Any time anyone mentions another person say, "I heard that they were dead."

34- Repeat the following conversation a dozen times: "Do you hear that?" "What?" "Never mind it's gone now."

35- Wander around the restaurant asking other diners for their parsley.

36- Leave tips in Bolivian currency.

37- Demand that everyone address you as "Conquistador".

38- Push all the flat Lego pieces together tightly.

39- At the laundromat, use one dryer for each of your socks.

40- When Christmas carolling, sing"Jingle Bells, Batman Smells" until physically restrained.

41- Wear a cape that says "Magnificent One".

42- As much as possible, skip rather than walk.

43- Stand over someone's shoulder, mumbling, as they read.

44- Finish the 99 bottles of beer song.

45- Sing the "This is the song that never ends..." song.

46- Leave your turn signal on for fifty miles.

47- Pretend your mouse is a CB radio and talk into it.

48- Drive half a block.

49- Name your dog "Dog".

50- Inform others that they exist only in your imagination.

51- Ask people what gender they are.

52- Try playing the William Tell Overture by tapping on the bottom of your chin.

When nearly done, announce "no, wait, I messed it up" and repeat.

53- Reply to everything someone says with "That's what YOU think."

54- Lick the filling out of all the Oreos, and place the cookie parts back in the tray.

55- Cultivate a Norwegian accent. If Norwegian, affect a Southern Drawl.

56- Forget the punchline to a long joke, but assure the listener it was a "real hoot".

57- Follow a few paces behind someone spraying everything they touch with a can of Lysol.

58- Deliberately hum songs that will remain lodged in co-workers' brains, such as the Archie's "Sugar", Mr. Rogers theme song and the 'Food Emporium' jingle. (If you haven't heard of Food Emporium, ask someone else.)

59- Lie obviously about trivial things such as the time of day.

60- Change your name to John Aaaaasmith for the great glory of being the first in the phonebook. Claim it's a Hawaiian name and demand that people pronounce each A.

61- Sit in your front yard pointing a hair dryer at passing cars.

62- Chew on pens that you borrowed.

63- Invent nonsense computer jargon in conversations, and see if people play along to avoid the appearance of ignorance.

64- Sing along at the opera.

65- Ask the waitress for an extra seat for your invisible friend.

66- Wear a LOT of cologne.

67- Listen to 33rpm records at 45rpm, and claim the faster speed is necessary because of your "superior mental processing".

68- Go to a poetry recital and ask why each poem doesn't rhyme.

69- Ask your co-workers mysterious questions, and scribble their answers in a notebook. Mutter something about “psychological profiles.”

70- Stare at static on the TV and claim you can see a "magic picture".

71- Select the same song on the jukebox fifty times.

72- Scuff your feet on a dry, shaggy carpet and seek out victims.

73- Do not add any inflection to the end of your sentences, giving the impression that you'll be saying more at any moment, leaving awkward silences.

74- Never make eye contact.

75- Never break eye contact.

76- Signal that a conversation is over by clamping your hands over your ears.

77- Make beeping noises when a large person backs up.

78- Leave your Christmas lights up and lit until September.

79- Inform your fiancees family that you can "burp" the alphabet, and begin to.

80- Every time you call somebody begin the conversation with, "Who is this?"

81- Construct your own "tricorder" and scan people with it, announcing the results.

82- Give a play-by-play account of a person's every action in a nasal Howard Cosell voice.

83- Holler random numbers while someone is counting.

92- If you have a glass eye, tap on it occasionally with your pen while talking to others.

93- Stomp on little plastic ketchup packets.

94- Insist on keeping your car windshield wipers running in all weather conditions, "to keep them tuned up."

95- Highlight irrelevant information on scientific papers and "cc." them to your boss.

96- Finish all your sentences, “In accordance with prophesy . . . “

97- While making presentations, bob your head like a parakeet.

98- Honk and wave to strangers.

99- Practice making fax and modem noises.

100- Disassemble your pen and “accidentally” flip the ink cartridge across the room.

14 THINGS TO DO IN A WAL-MART WHILE YOUR SIGNIFICANT OTHER IS TAKING THEIR SWEET TIME SHOPPING!

AUTHOR UNKNOWN

1. Get 24 boxes of condoms & randomly put them in people's carts when they aren't looking

2. Set all the alarm clocks in housewares to go off at 5 minute intervals.

3. Make a trail of tomato juice on the floor to the rest rooms.

4. Walk up to an employee and tell him/her in an official tone, "Code 3 in housewares," and see what happens.

5. Go to the Service Desk and ask to put a bag of M&M's on layaway.

6. Move a 'CAUTION - WET FLOOR' sign to a carpeted area.

7. Set up a tent in the camping department and tell other shoppers you'll invite them in only if they bring pillows from the bedding department.

8. When a clerk asks if they can help you, begin to cry and ask, "Why can't you people just leave me alone?"

9. While handling guns in the hunting department ask the clerk if he knows where the antidepressants are.

10. Dart around the store suspiciously while loudly humming the theme from Mission Impossible."

11. In the auto department, practice your Madonna look using different size funnels.

12. Hide in the clothing rack and when people browse through say, "PICK ME! PICK ME!"

13. When an announcement comes over the loud speaker, assume the fetal position and scream, "NO! NO! It's those voices again."

And last but not least,...

14. Go into a fitting room and yell loudly, "Hey! We're out of toilet paper in here!"

WHAT STORE EMPLOYEES REALLY MEAN

AUTHOR UNKNOWN

1. "Can I help you get a size?"
(Don't touch that, I just spent an hour folding it and I don't need your hands messing it up again.)

2. "Do you need help with anything?"
(Quick, my manager is coming around the corner and I need to look busy.)

3. "Welcome to (Store Name Here)"
(Good, another customer to mess up my entire store just to buy a pair of socks.)

4. "Have a nice day!"
(Now that you ruined mine.)

5. "Thank you for shopping at (Store Name Here)"
(Thanks for emptying your wallet with us!)

6. "Do you need a shopping cart to help you carry your items?"
(The more you can carry, the more you can buy!)

7. "I love your shirt! Where did you get it?"
(Your shirt is much nicer than the clothes we sell here. Why are you even shopping here?)

8. "Can I help you get something down?"
(I'll get a ladder and put it up for you since this other nice customer put in the absolute wrong place.)

9. "Don't worry about folding it, I can do it"
(You would just mess it up again if you folded it.)

10. "No, we don't have any more in the back"
(I just don't want to check.)

INNER STRENGTH

AUTHOR UNKNOWN

If you can start the day without caffeine or pep pills,
If you can be cheerful, ignoring aches and pains,
If you can resist complaining and boring people with your troubles,
If you can eat the same food everyday and be grateful for it,
If you can understand when loved ones are too busy to give you time,
If you can overlook when people take things out on you when, through no fault of yours, something goes wrong,
If you can take criticism and blame without resentment,
If you can face the world without lies and deceit,
If you can conquer tension without medical help,
If you can relax without liquor,
If you can sleep without the aid of drugs,
If you can do all these things,
Then you are probably the family dog.

-14-

WISDOM

QUOTES ON WISDOM

Suppose that we are wise enough to learn and know -- and yet not wise enough to control our learning and knowledge, so that we use it to destroy ourselves? Even if that is so, knowledge remains better than ignorance. It is better to know -- even if the knowledge endures only for the moment that comes before destruction -- than to gain eternal life at the price of a dull and swinish lack of comprehension of a universe that swirls unseen before us in all its wonder. That was the choice of Achilles, and it is mine, too.
Isaac Asimov

Do not seek to follow in the footsteps of the wise. Seek what they sought.
Basho

Wise men still seek Him today.
Dan Bell

The live in wisdom who see themselves in all and all in them, who have renounced every selfish desire and sense craving tormenting the heart.
Bhagavad Gita

In much wisdom is much grief; and he that increaseth knowledge increaseth sorrow.
The Bible

The testimony of the Lord is sure making wise the simple.
Psalms 19:7

Through wisdom is a house built; and by understanding it is established; and by knowledge shall every room be filled with precious and pleasant riches.
The Bible

The price of wisdom is eternal thought.
Frank Birch

What is the price of experience? Do men buy it for a song? Or wisdom for a dance in the street? No, it is bought with the price of all the man hath, his house, his wife, his children.
William Blake

True wisdom lies in gathering the precious things out of each day as it goes by.
E. S. Bouton

Time ripens all things; no man is born wise.
Miguel De Cervantes

A wise man thinks what is easy is difficult.
John Churton Collins

Knowledge comes, but wisdom lingers. It may not be difficult to store up in the mind a vast quantity of face within a comparatively short time, but the ability to form judgments requires the severe discipline of hard work and the tempering heat of experience and maturity.
Calvin Coolidge

Raphael paints wisdom; Handel sings it, Phidias carves it, Shakespeare writes it, Wren builds it, Columbus sails it, Luther preaches it, Washington arms it, Watt mechanizes it.
Ralph Waldo Emerson

Wisdom is like electricity. There is no permanently wise man, but men capable of wisdom, who, being put into certain company, or other favorable conditions, become wise for a short time, as glasses rubbed acquire electric power for a while.
Ralph Waldo Emerson

Wisdom is knowing when to speak your mind and when to mind your speech.
Evangel

Where there is charity and wisdom, there is neither fear nor ignorance. Where there is patience and humility, there is neither anger nor vexation. Where there is poverty and joy, there is neither greed nor avarice. Where there is peace and meditation, there is neither anxiety nor doubt.
St. Francis of Assisi

The doors of wisdom are never shut.
Benjamin Franklin

Just as a cautious businessman avoids investing all his capital in one concern, so wisdom would probably admonish us also not to anticipate all our happiness from one quarter alone.
Sigmund Freud

TIME GETS BETTER WITH AGE

AUTHOR UNKNOWN

I learned that I like my teacher because she cries when we sing "Silent Night". -Age 5

I learned that our dog doesn't want to eat my broccoli *either.* -Age 7

I learned that when I wave to people *in the country*, they stop what they are doing and wave back. -Age 9

I learned that just when I get my room the way I like it, Mom makes me clean it up again. -Age 12

I learned that if you want to cheer yourself up, you should *try cheering someone else* up. -Age 14

I learned that although it's hard to admit it, I'm secretly glad my parents are strict with me. -Age 15

I learned that silent company is often more healing than words of advice. -Age 24

I learned that brushing my child's hair is one of life's great pleasures. -Age 26

I learned that wherever I go, the world's worst drivers have followed me there. -Age 29

I learned that if someone says something unkind about me, I must live so that no one will believe it. -Age 30

I learned that there are people who love you dearly but just don't know how to show it. -Age 42

I learned that you can make some one's day by simply sending them a little note. -Age 44

I learned that the greater a persons sense of guilt, the greater his or her need to cast blame on others. -Age 46

I learned that children and *grand*parents are natural allies. -Age 47

I learned that no matter what happens, or how bad it seems today, life does go on, and it will be better tomorrow. -Age 48

I learned that singing "Amazing Grace" can lift my spirits for hours. -Age 49

I learned that motel mattresses are better on the side away from the phone. -Age 50

I learned that you can tell a lot about a man by the way he handles these three things: a rainy day, lost luggage, and tangled Christmas tree lights. -Age 51

I learned that keeping a vegetable garden is worth a medicine cabinet full of pills. -Age 52

I learned that regardless of your relationship with your parents, you miss them terribly after they die. -Age 53

I learned that making a living is not the same thing as making a life. -Age 58

I learned that if you want to do something positive for your children, work to improve your marriage. -Age 61

I learned that life sometimes gives you a second chance. -Age 62

I learned that you shouldn't go through life with a catcher's mitt on both hands. You need to be able to throw something back. -Age 64

I learned that if you *pursue* happiness, it will elude you. But if you focus on your family, the needs of others, your work, meeting new people, and doing the very best you can, happiness will find you. -Age 65

I learned that whenever I decide something with kindness, I usually make the right decision. -Age 66

I learned that everyone can use a prayer. -Age 72

I learned that even when I have pains, I don't have to be one. -Age 82

I learned that every day you should reach out and touch someone. People love that human touch-holding hands, a warm hug, or just a friendly pat on the back. -Age 90

I learned that I still have a lot to learn. -Age 92

I learned that you should pass this on to someone you care about. Sometimes they just need a little something to make them smile.

GREAT TRUTHS ABOUT GROWING OLD

AUTHOR UNKNOWN

Growing old is mandatory; growing up is optional.

Forget the health food. I need all the preservatives I can get.

When you fall down, you wonder what else you can do while you're down there.

You're getting old when you get the same sensation from a rocking chair that you once got from a roller coaster.

It's frustrating when you know all the answers, but nobody bothers to ask you the questions.

Time may be a great healer, but it's a lousy beautician.

Wisdom comes with age, but sometimes age comes alone.

Things I've Learned . . . .

AUTHOR UNKNOWN

I've learned....
that the best classroom in the world
is at the feet of an elderly person.

I've learned....
that when you're in love, it shows.

I've learned....
that just one person saying to me,
"You've made my day!" makes my day.

I've learned....
that I feel better about myself when
I make others feel better about themselves.

I've learned....
that having a child fall asleep in your
arms is one of the most peaceful
feelings in the world.

I've learned....
that what we have done for ourselves
alone dies with us. What we have done
for others and the world remains and
is immortal.

I've learned....
that one sincere apology is worth more
than all the roses money can buy.

I've learned....
that words harshly spoken are as difficult
to retrieve as feathers in a gale.

I've learned....
that being kind is more important than
being right.

I've learned....
that you should never say no to a
gift from a child.

I've learned....
that I can always pray for someone when
I don't have the strength to help him
in some other way.

I've learned....
that no matter how serious your life
requires you to be, everyone needs a
friend to act goofy with.

I've learned....
that sometimes all a person needs is a
hand to hold and a heart to understand.

WISDOM FOR THE ROAD

AUTHOR UNKNOWN

Cherish things while you still have them, before they're gone,
and you realize how precious they really are.

Life can only be understood backwards,
but it must be lived forwards.

Everything in life is temporary.
So if things are going good,
enjoy it because it won't last forever.

And if things are going bad,
don't worry because it won't last forever either.

Destiny is not a matter of chance,
it is a matter of choice;
it is not a thing to be waited for,
it is a thing to be achieved.

A journey of a thousand miles
begins with a single step.

Never cross a bridge
without knowing how to swim the tides.
If you could not add years to your life
Add life to your years.

WHAT I LEARNED

AUTHOR UNKNOWN

I've learned –
That you cannot make someone love you. All you can do is be someone who can be loved. The rest is up to them.

I've learned –
that no matter how much I care, some people just don't care back.

I've learned –
that it takes years to build up trust, and only seconds to destroy it.

I've learned –
that it's not what you have in your life but who you have in your life that counts.

I've learned –
that you can get by on charm for about fifteen minutes. After that, you'd better know something.

I've learned –
that it's not what happens to people that's important. It's what they do about it.

I've learned –
that you can do something in an instant that will give you heartache for life.

I've learned –
that you should always leave loved ones with loving words. It may be the last time you see them.

I've learned –
that either you control your attitude or it controls you.

I've learned –
that regardless of how hot and steamy a relationship is at first, the passion fades and there had better be something else to take its place.

I've learned –
that learning to forgive takes practice.

I've learned –
that money is a lousy way of keeping score.

I've learned –
that sometimes when I'm angry I have the right to be angry, but that doesn't give me the right to be cruel.

I've learned –
that true friendship continues to grow, even over the longest distance. Same goes for true love.

I've learned –
that maturity has more to do with what types of experiences you've had and what you've learned from them and less to do with how many years you've lived.

I've learned –
that you should never tell a child their dreams are unlikely or outlandish. Few things are more humiliating, and what a tragedy it would be if they believed you.

I've learned –
that no matter how good a friend is, they're going to hurt you every once in a while and you must forgive them for that.

I've learned –
that it isn't always enough to be forgiven by others.
Sometimes you have to learn to forgive yourself.

I've learned –
that no matter how bad your heart is broken the world doesn't stop for your grief.

I've learned –
that just because two people argue, it doesn't mean they don't love each other and just because they don't argue, it doesn't mean they do.

I've learned –
that sometimes you have to put the individual ahead of their actions.

I've learned –
that you shouldn't be so eager to find out a secret. It could change your life forever.

I've learned –
that no matter how you try to protect your children, they will eventually get hurt and you will hurt in the process.

I've learned –
that there are many ways of falling and staying in love.

I've learned –
that your life can be changed in a matter of hours by people who don't even know you.

I've learned –
that even when you think you have no more to give, when a friend cries out to you, you will find the strength to help.

I've learned –
that writing, as well as talking, can ease emotional pains.

I've learned –
that credentials on the wall do not make you a decent human being.

I've learned –
that the people you care most about in life are taken from you too soon.

-14-

DEATH

QUOTES ON DEATH

Death is better, a milder fate than tyranny.
Aeschylus

Do not fear death so much, but rather the inadequate life.
Bertolt Brecht

For certain is death for the born
And certain is birth for the dead;
Therefore over the inevitable
Thou shouldst not grieve.
Bhagavad Gita

Death is nothing to us, since when we are, death has not come, and when death has come, we are not.
Epicurus

Life does not cease to be funny when people die any more than it ceases to be serious when people laugh.
George Bernard Shaw

There is no cure for birth and death save to enjoy the interval.
George Santayana

Pale Death with impartial tread beats at the poor man's cottage door and at the palaces of kings.
Horace

A single death is a tragedy; a million deaths is a statistic.
Joseph Stalin

The dead cannot cry out for justice; it is a duty of the living to do so for them.
Lois McMaster Bujold

Think not disdainfully of death, but look on it with favor; for even death is one of the things that Nature wills.
Marcus Aurelius Antoninus

The report of my death was an exaggeration.
Mark Twain

Never knock on Death's door: ring the bell and run away! Death really hates that!
Matt Frewer

Must not all things at the last be swallowed up in death?
Plato

As men, we are all equal in the presence of death.
Publilius Syrus

The fear of death is more to be dreaded than death itself.
Publilius Syrus

If I could drop dead right now, I'd be the happiest man alive.
Samuel Goldwyn

Dying is a very dull, dreary affair. And my advice to you is to have nothing whatever to do with it.
W. Somerset Maugham

Life isn't fair. It's just fairer than death, that's all.
William Goldman, "The Princess Bride"

WHEN TOMORROW STARTS WITHOUT ME

AUTHOR UNKNOWN

When tomorrow starts without me and I'm not there to see...
If the sun should rise and find your eyes all filled with tears for me.
I wish so much you wouldn't cry the way you did today,
While thinking of the many things we didn't get to say.

I know how much you love me; As much as I love you,
And each time that you think of me, I know you'll miss me too.
But when tomorrow starts without me, please try to understand,
That an angel came and called my name and took me by the hand.

He said my place was ready in heaven far above,
And that I'd have to leave behind all those I dearly love.
But as I turned to walk away, a tear fell from my eye.
For all my life, I'd always thought, I didn't want to die.
I had so much to live for; So much left yet to do;
It seemed almost impossible that I was leaving you.
I thought of all the yesterdays, the good ones and the bad,

I thought of all the love we shared and all the fun we had.

If I could relive yesterday, Just even for a while...
I'd say good-bye and kiss you and maybe see you smile.
But then I fully realized, that this could never be,
For emptiness and memories would take the place of me.

And when I thought of worldly things I might miss come tomorrow,
I thought of you, and when I did, My heart was filled with sorrow.

But when I walked through heaven's gates, I felt so much at home
When God looked down and smiled at me, from His great golden throne.

He said, "This is eternity, all that I've promised you.

Today your life on earth is past, but here life starts anew.
I promise no tomorrow and today will always last,
And since each day's the very same, there's no longing for the past."

"You have been so faithful, so trusting and so true.

Though there were times you did some things you knew you shouldn't do.
But you have been forgiven and now at last you're free.
So won't you come and take my hand and share my life with me?"

So, when tomorrow starts without me, don't think we're far apart,

For every time you think of me, I'm right here, in your heart.

ABOUT THE AUTHOR

Russ Ulmer lives in Underwood Iowa with his wife, Janice and two children, Matthew and Elizabeth. He is a writer, computer problem solver, part-time coach, parent, housekeeper, taxi driver and homework helper….and oh yes, he also has a full time job. He can be reached by email at ulmerfour@walnutel.net or by calling (402) 639-7427.

Visit our website: www.insightsonlife.net

Russ Ulmer is available for public appearances. Having a fundraising program? Russ is always willing to be a part of your fundraiser, sign books and donate a portion of book sales to your organization. $5 from every book sold will be donated to your charity. Just contact us by phone or email.

CONTRIBUTIONS WANTED

Future *Insights* books are in the works and your contributions are appreciated. We will be putting together books on Nursing, Teaching, Motherhood, Fatherhood, Children, Love, and Money. We reserve the right to edit material.

If you'd like to contribute a story (humorous or serious), quote or poem, send them to:

Insights Publishing
Attn: Russ Ulmer
PO Box 7
Underwood, IA 51576

OR Email to: ulmerfour@walnutel.net